Shirley —
Good Readings
&
Best Wishes
John P. Eggers
1/7/96
39/200

 **Greetings From Waterville, Minn.**

The above photo is from a **Backman** Produce Calendar dated 1950. This is the Waterville that I knew. There's **Luther's** on the corner of Main and Third Street. I see the old schoolhouse with that big gym. The furniture factory is present but no longer in business. **Dudley's** Red Owl is still in the **Haase** Building and the lot where the Commercial Hotel stood is still vacant.

If you look really close, you can see my brother, **Craig, Roland Bittrich** and me chasing a chicken that escaped from **Backman's**.

 Greetings From Waterville, Minn.

Greetings From Waterville, Minn.

A postcard history of Waterville and much more

John R. Eggers
1996

Robert Rausch was re-elected chairman of the school board. Edgar Eggers was re-elected treasurer. (1956)

Greetings From Waterville, Minn.

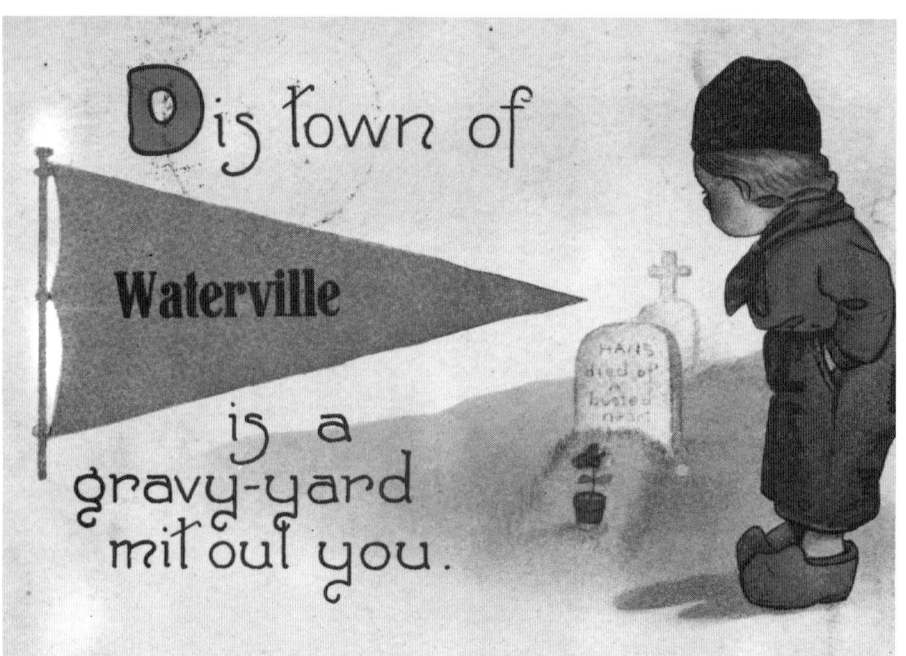

Wagon wheels and Waterville wives

Alex Blye is looking out of his wagon shop door and wondering when the photographer will be through so he can get back to work. The Waterville Furniture Factory has been shipping large quantities of furniture and they are badly in need of wagons. Depot patrons have been complaining of an almost continuous blockade of the depot platform.

It's 1886 and **Miss Ida Oblinger** has gone to Hutchinson to attend school. **Alex** helped get her father's rig ready to take her to the train station.

Mr. Farthing and **Mr. Timpane** are in need of a couple of new wheels on their rigs. They are both running for County Commissioner. **Alex** figured it would be a good idea to locate his shop next to City Hall on Second Street and he was right. He won't admit it but it was actually **Mrs. Blye's** idea.

Greetings From Waterville, Minn.
Copyright © 1996 by John R. Eggers
All rights reserved.
Printed in the United States of America.
No part of this book may be used or reproduced in any manner whatsoever without written permission except in the case of brief quotations embodied in critical articles or reviews. For information: Envisioning Your Future, 3024 Sunnyside Dr., NE, Bemidji, Minnesota 56601 (218) 751-0179

ISBN 1-888954-01-9

Printed by
Arrow Printing
1375 Washington Ave. S.
Bemidji, MN 56601

Notify Don Werner if you are interested in the Waterama Boat parade to held July 3,4,5. (1959)

This book is dedicated to my parents Edgar and Helen Eggers

My mother, **Helen**, was born in the house just west of St. Peter's (Bell) Church in 1919. At the time, it served as the parsonage for the Bell Church parochial school teacher, her father, **John Raedeke**. After graduating from Jordan High School, she came to Waterville in 1937 and never left.

My father, **Edgar**, was born in Reeder, North Dakota in 1917. He came to Waterville in 1925 when his father, the **Reverend Henry F. Eggers**, received a call to be pastor of the Trinity Lutheran Church. My father never left Waterville once he arrived.

> **Mom worked at Roemhildt's cafe when you could get a complete dinner for 25 cents.**

> **Dad is very proud of the Eggers Prairie located east of Waterville—land that has never been tilled.**

Mom and Dad were married in August of 1940.

Mom worked at **Charlie Roemhildt's** cafe (now the site of the Pizza Palace and formerly **Stucky's** Pharmacy) when you could get a complete dinner for 25 cents. She later worked at **John Dudley's** Red Owl where ten pounds of sugar would be on sale for 89 cents.

Dad worked at **Schomel's** grocery store located in the **Bill Haase** building that was situated on the north side of Main Street between 1st and 2nd streets. He worked there while attending high school. After graduation he began work at Citizens State Bank in 1937 and retired from there in 1977. He also served as the bookkeeper for **Luther's** Ben Franklin and **Worlein's** Furniture and did income tax, which he still does today.

You can see that both my brother, **Craig**, and I came from a family who knew the meaning of work.

Both of my parents are well. My mother enjoys playing bridge. Although she would never admit it, she probably has the cleanest home in town. My dad is a real outdoors person. He fishes and hunts and takes care of his lawn. He is very proud of the **Eggers'** Prairie located east of Waterville—land that has never been tilled. Can you imagine?

I have always said to myself that if I were to be born at another time it would have been during the same era when Mom and Dad were born. They were young during the roaring 20's, experienced the depression, lived through World War II, contributed to the baby boom era and made it through the sixties. That's a lot of living and a lot of stories.

Perhaps, more than any other reason, it's the stories that have motivated me to write this book and preserve some of the history that caused my parents to want to remain in Waterville.

This book is a gift to my parents. I wrote it with them in mind. Waterville has meant a lot to me in my life but I know it means a lot more to my parents.

> **I wrote it with them in mind. Waterville has meant a lot to me in my life but I know it means a lot more to my parents.**

Edgar and Helen Eggers Craig and John 1945

Florence Rogers is valedictorian at WHS. (1886)

Greetings From Waterville, Minn.

Forewords

I know some of the history of Waterville. It will be fun to reminisce about fun times that we had in Waterville and see some of the old pictures and different businesses that were in our town.

I'll enjoy reading John's book.

Dorothy Bittrich

(One of the best parts of my life was growing up in west Waterville. The **Honken's, Fonken's, Harriman's, Roemhildt's, Anderson's, Grobe's, Scholer's, Rimer's, and Bittrich's** were all part of my extended family. My brother **Craig** and I spent as much time at the **Walter** and **Dorothy Bittrich** home as we did our own home. If Waterville were to select a "nice person" award, it would go to **Mrs. Dorothy Bittrich**. "**Mrs. Bittrich**, thanks for always being so nice.")

I deem it an honor and a privilege to write a foreword on schooling in Waterville to **Dr. Eggers'** *Greetings From Waterville, Minn.*

I have known **Dr. Eggers** since he first came into my 10th grade history class. He was also my quarterback on the football team.

I was a high school history instructor and coach for 33 years. Thirty of those years were here in Waterville where I still reside. After my teaching career I also served on the Board of Education and am still active on committees to better our educational system.

I always felt, and still do, that we had an excellent education system here at Waterville, which later became known as Waterville-Elysian and now known as Waterville-Elysian-Morristown Public Schools.

Our system laid the foundation for many students who later became successful doctors, lawyers, farmers, teachers, businessmen, and employees of many different job ventures.

It is my sincere hope that the educational system we have had will continue for many decades to come.

Dr. Eggers is to be commended for all his time and effort in putting this booklet together.

Ernest Dahl

(When I think of all of my teachers I enjoyed at Waterville during my entire elementary and secondary schooling years, **Mr. Dahl's** name comes to mind. He was characterized by his students as a "tough" teacher, a teacher who had high expectations. His dedication to education and, in particular, to Waterville Schools, is one of the reasons I selected **Mr. Dahl** to write a foreword. The other reason is that I was never really satisfied with my history term paper and even though it is a bit late, I hope he will allow me to exchange this project for the one I turned in 35 years ago.)

What fun it is to learn of the interests, activities and concerns of past generations in a community which has been a part of our lives.

This book will contribute to the appreciation of the natural beauty of Waterville and to an increased bond with the past, present, and future.

Readers will find interesting information and pleasant memories as they travel through the years in words and pictures.

Anna Fay Fritz

(They would meet on many occasions throughout the year but I suppose the most important gathering took place every New Year's day at the farm home of **Earl and Anna Fay Fritz**. The Pot Luck bunch consisting of **Jack** and **Harriet Backman**, **Edgar** and **Helen Eggers**, **Glenn** and **Molly Preuss**, **Harold** and **Grace Preuss**, **Bob** and **Mabel Rausch**, **Art** and **Sylvia Roeglin** and all of the kids would gather at the **Fritz** home and watch the Rose Bowl game, eat a lot and just have fun. The Pot Luck bunch that remains today still meets on occasion. All of the kids are scattered now but one of my fondest memories of Waterville will always be the Pot Luck bunch. They were the next best thing to a favorite relative that would come to visit but never stay a long time. More importantly, the Pot Luck bunch always brought along something to eat and drink.)

Florence Rogers Glotfelter passes away—Waterville's oldest native citizen. (1955)

Forewords Continued

History is an exciting and fascinating topic. Its preservation for posterity is vital. *Greetings From Waterville, Minn.* captures the flavor of the first hundred years of Waterville in words and pictures.

Those of us who are living the second hundred years need only recall how frequently we say, "So-and-so lived there," or "Such-and-such used to be located there" to realize that the past is part of us. It is important that we preserve it.

Larry Meskan

(As Mayor of Waterville, **Larry Meskan** represents those individuals past and present who have provided the leadership that has resulted in making Waterville a nice place to live and learn and work. **Mr. Meskan** was also a Civics teacher of mine who proclaimed that hockey was the most exciting sport to watch and play. You see, I still remember some things he taught me.)

From this resort owner's viewpoint, the depth of **Dr. Eggers'** book reveals his love for his hometown beginning. Inspired by his family ties in Waterville, he takes us on a nostalgic stroll through tourism's birth in this small town to the present time.

Tourism in Waterville's 50-plus lake area has had a remarkable impact on this southern Minnesota community's economy and with the emergence of the "seasonal camper" from the mid 80's to the present, the beautiful lakes continue to be the main attraction.

Though the resort life is rewarded with family togetherness, past and present operators often sense the real opportunities in this area remain untapped. This thought has been passed down through three generations of resort owners in my family, from Grandfather **Otto Pope** (1917-1955) to me (1955-1995), to my son, **Nyl Pope** (1990 - forward).

Del Pope

(People who visit Waterville do so with one thing in mind—to fish and to have fun. **Del Pope** is a lifetime resident of Waterville who took advantage of Waterville's resources and provided a place where families could do just that. The tourist business remains an important and strong part of Waterville's economy. As **Del Pope** inferred in his foreward, the future looks bright for Waterville. The **Pope** family has played a significant part in its past and, no doubt, will play a significant part in its future.)

Greetings From Waterville, Minn., an interesting title to pique anyone's thoughts about life in general or in small town America.

All of us who have grown up in rural areas can relate and enjoy reminiscing about their younger days, their families, their schools, their jobs, and their history.

This pictorial book will bring back memories to everyone; enjoyable memories where people can say, " I remember when."

Dr. Eggers has favored all of us with this undertaking. I plan to send this to my children, friends and relatives.

Bill Rieke

(**Bill Rieke** is a member of my high school graduating class and a life long friend. He and I sat next to each other on the bench on **Guy Kelly's** basketball team. We also roomed together in college (along with **Eddie Stangler**) and worked together at **Dudley's** Red Owl. I wanted **Bill** to write a forward for two reasons: first as a member of the WHS class of '61 and second as the son of **Dr. Lowell Rieke**, one of Waterville's most favored citizens. If Waterville were to have a citizen's hall of fame, **Doc Rieke** would be a charter inductee. **Doc** and his wife, **Janet,** will be long remembered for helping to make Waterville a better place to live.)

Norman and Laura (Glotfelter) Findahl purchased a 640 acre farm north of town. (1940's)

Forewords Continued

Having lived in the Waterville area and having been acquainted with many happenings over 40 years I find it very interesting to learn more of Waterville's history. *Greetings From Waterville, Minn.* brings that history to life and one can reminisce on Waterville's past. Documentation of that past is important for future generations. Although I have been only a small part of Waterville history, my retirement has been a joy in the "Bullhead Capitol of the World." Reading this book you will see the need for such documentation and enjoy looking forward to the future of Waterville. **John Eggers** deserves a "thank you" for writing it.

Pastor Victor Roth

(**Pastor Roth** has been a significant part of the **Eggers** family ever since he came to town to be pastor of Trinity Lutheran upon my grandfather's [**Rev. Henry F. Eggers**] retirement. He not only was a fine pastor, he also was, and still is, an active person in the community life of Waterville. He was around to console the **Eggers** family on the deaths of my grandparents, uncle **Roger Eggers** and great uncle **Fred Vogel**. **Pastor Roth** is an important part of Waterville's religious history and I was delighted to ask him to write a foreword for this book.)

I'm looking forward to **Dr. John Eggers'** book *Greetings From Waterville, Minn.*

The history of Waterville is rich with memories for me. My grandfather, **Wick Beach**, was born in 1859 in the Waterville area. My mother, **Lucinda Beach** and father, **Frank P. Luker**, were both born here, too. So, I grew up hearing the stories and experiencing the changes in the area.

In 1919, my folks purchased the farm with **Andrews** Opera race horse barn and track. They later developed a summer resort on the property—Tetonka Homes.

Greetings from Waterville, Minn. will help preserve our history and remind people of the beauty of "home."

Mary Lou Luker Solyntjes

(**Mary Lou** is someone that could and should write a more complete history of Waterville. She helped me be honest on many of the facts and names and places. I enjoyed visiting with **Mary Lou** and her husband, **Herman**. Both have a lot of information tucked away in their minds and a lot of stories—and they're both still young. Think of the stories they will be able to tell when people begin referring to them as "old timers.")

I have lived all 83 years of my life in Waterville. I think that everyone likes to talk about "old times" and to look at old pictures that are of places they remember. Our four children ask about the "Good Ole Days" all the time. *Greetings From Waterville, Minn.* will help our "Ole Times" live on. We will be able to pass this book to our children and their children. And new families who move to Waterville will be able to read about the history of their new home.

Mabel Walz

(**Mabel Walz** is Waterville's official secretary and has been since her kids were in school. If there is anything you need to know about Waterville in the last 50 years, **Mabel** can tell you. Her daughter, **Clara**, graduated with me and was a high school cheerleader for the Waterville Buccaneers. **Mary Ann, Donna, Clara** and **Billy** were outstanding students for WHS. They took pride in their school and the school took pride in them. No doubt, **Mabel** and **Mickey** had a lot to do with this.)

For those of us who lived in Waterville most of our lives and then moved away, it is still and always will be our "home town." "Home" has a connotation of love, warmth, support, fun, dear friends, etc. This book is a treasury of memories like that. My sincere thanks to Dr. John R. Eggers.

Sylvia Roeglin Hoehle

(**Sylvia** is a very close friend of the **Eggers** family and a graduate of Waterville High School. Mom worked with **Sylvia** in her father's cafe (**Roemhildt's** Cafe), played bridge with her, went to the same church and together enjoyed the fun of the "pot luck" bunch. **Sylvia** represents those citizens of Waterville who moved away but takes a special interest in the "goings-on" of her home town.)

Oscar Spooner is remodeling his residence. He put in new windows and a new front porch. (1929)

Greetings From Waterville, Minn.

Hugs and kisses and a lot of thanks to the good people who helped with this book.

Howard Anderson
Leona Anderson
James Baumgartner
Dorothy Bittrich
Doris Butterfield
Shirley Cook
Cleveland C. Cram
Ernest Dahl
John Dudley
Sister Charlotte Dusbabek
Craig and Janice Eggers
Edgar and Helen Eggers
Henry Fessel
Anna Fay Fritz
Carollea Gilomen
Evelyn Gregor
Joan Gregor
Bernadine Hildebrant
Gerry Hrdlicka
John "Fred" Hrdlicka
Beatrice Hayes Hedges
Elaine Herbig
Sylvia Hoehle
Bob and Larene Kerr
Jack Luther
Mae C. Mach
Barb Mader
Dorothy Mager
Lois O. Meschke
Larry and Marlys Meskan
Ted Messal
Nancy Minks
Jeannette Morris
Adeline Nierenz
Sally Backman Olson
Verna Olson
Patricia Remington Oppert
Seth Osborn
Charles Pittmann
Del Pope

Inez Pope
Gene Preuss
Marilyn Ringheim
Dorothy Roemhildt
Victor Roth
Uzada Salmon
Nancy Sheehy
Betty Schwartz
Donovan Schwichtenberg
Melvin Schulz
Loretta Shefland

Helen Spooner
Herman Solyntjes
Maxine Svela
Robert Townsend
Monica Traxler
Clarice Trotter
Lyle Vail
Jack Webster
Donna Wilmes
Audrey Westgate
Agnes Wetzel

Mary Lou Solyntjes and Mabel Walz

A very special thanks to **Mary Lou Solyntjes** and **Mabel Walz** for their help in reading various sections of the book and sitting and visiting with me about the history of our home town. Like so many Waterville people, **Mary Lou** and **Mabel** are very kind people. Thank you.

Kathleen Janice Piwinski Eggers

Kathy has never lived in Waterville but she knows almost as much about it as I do. **Kathy**, my wife, was born in Detroit, Michigan in 1943. She graduated from the University of Michigan in 1965 and entered the Peace Corps the same year. I entered the Peace Corps in the same year and in the same program. It took the girl from the big city about a year before she noticed the boy from the Bullhead Capitol. How do you figure? You should be glad that she did because this book would never have been written without her help, guidance and encouragement.

Kathy inherited the quality of detail from her mother and father **Ann** and **Stan Piwinski**. Her creative qualities come from her sister, **Barb Piwinski**. With **Kathy's** help, I have tried to incorporate both detail and creativity in this book of a history of a small town in Minnesota.

We were married in 1968 in Livonia, Michigan. After 28 years of marriage we are still learning about each other. "It's the song you sing and the smile you wear that's making the sunshine everywhere." James Whitcomb Riley's verse is fitting of **Kathy**. It's not **Kathy's** singing but just her presence that makes me smile—everywhere. Te quiero, **Katie**.

Fishing is in full blast. The Cannon River is lined with fishermen. (1909)

Introduction to *Greetings From Waterville, Minn.*

I began leaving Waterville in 1961 to attend college and I have been coming home to Waterville ever since. **In many ways this book represents a way for both you and me to come home to Waterville.**

Waterville is mentioned often in my writing, teaching and public speaking. Perhaps, the reason why it means so much to me is that it is always there to come home to. People need constants in their lives and Waterville has been a constant in my life.

The book is intended to be a walk through Waterville during the early 1900's and into the fifties. It is not intended to be a play by play description of its formal history although it does contain a brief history of Waterville. It also contains the names of many of its citizens and connects the name to a date and something of interest about that individual. Of course, it's the people that make a town a town no matter if they were a butcher, baker or candle stick maker.

Greetings From Waterville, Minn. is a pictorial history of Waterville using early postcards. Why only postcards? Real photo postcards were at the height of popularity between 1900-1925. Since the production of real photo postcards was limited to however many a photographer could sell locally, many scenes and subjects were made in very limited quantities and are rare.

Postcards represent histories of communities during their infancy as seen through the eyes of photographers. These early postcards document a city's growth. Without the initiative of these photographers (in this case, **Bert Ryan** and **Charles Christman**) much of the pictorial history of Waterville would have been lost.

> **The book is intended to be a walk through Waterville during the early 1900's and into the fifties.**

Even though Waterville is a small community and only one hundred and fifty years old, there is substantial information about the businesses, the resorts, and the people. The book could easily have been twice as long if I had wanted to use other non-postcard photos and all of the information provided to me. I already owned a significant number of Waterville postcards and I wanted a way of limiting the information. The solution was to use my postcard collection and information about whatever was depicted on the postcard. With some exceptions I have used other non-postcard photos in the book.

There has been some documentation of the history of Waterville. Several students of former Waterville High School history teacher, **Mr. Ernest Dahl**, devoted their senior history term paper to writing about Waterville. Information from the papers of **Leon Mager, Jr., Lyle Vail** and **Sally Backman Olson** was used as well as Waterville newspapers (*Sentinel, Advance, Lake Region Life*). As far as I am aware, there is no formal published history of Waterville. And, certainly no pictorial history of Waterville. All of the written literature I have gathered will, by the way, be donated to the Waterville Public Library.

In 1976 **Carol Morshing** and **Jim Hruska** did an excellent job of writing some historical vignettes as told by lake region residents. In their book, *Stepping Stones*, **Carol** and **Jim** preserved some good stories and photographs of Waterville and Elysian. Some of the information used in this book has come from *Stepping Stones*.

I purposely left some questionable data in the book—it might be a date, a place, or a face. This will cause you to look at and analyze the book extra closely. Should there be a second printing, this would be a good time to make the corrections.

I don't like to write anything unless it is interesting, fun, or entertaining. When you read *Greetings From Waterville, Minn.*, I hope it will be interesting, fun and entertaining for you. More importantly, I hope it will cause you to come home to Waterville.

> **Special note to readers:**
>
> **Keep a magnifying glass handy. Signs, faces, and notices are hidden by the naked eye but come to life with the help of a good glass. This advice isn't just for the "old timers."**

Dick Sutter landed a 22 pound carp while fishing on Lake Tetonka using a cane pole and a sunfish hook. (1959)

 Greetings From Waterville, Minn.

Greetings From Waterville, Minn.

Table of Contents

When you are in Waterville to enjoy our street opening celebration, stop in and say hello!

We hope you will take full pleasure from our new lights and hard surfaced streets

Security State Bank
Complete Banking Service
Waterville

Dedication
Forewords
Thank you
Introduction

Chapter 1: Let's go down town
Chapter 2: Waterville landmarks: Many are gone; some remain but aren't the same
Chapter 3: The Waterville bridges: places to drive to, drive on, fish from, jump from and hide under
Chapter 4: Fire, floods, fairs and other significant events
Chapter 5: "Keep the altar fires burning:" The churches of Waterville
Chapter 6: Waterville business and industry
Chapter 7: If you tell them, they will come: Waterville's resorts
Chapter 8: Waterville High School
Chapter 9: Watervillians: Where all of the women are gentle, all of the men are helpful and all of the children think they are above average
Chapter 10: Views of Waterville residences
Chapter 11: A brief history of Waterville
Chapter 12: I remember . . .
Chapter 13: Waterville: 2096

The large barn on the Roman Grubish home was moved several inches away from the silo by the windstorm. (1944)

 **Greetings From Waterville, Minn.**

No more dust and mud—Waterville in 1960

THURSDAY, OCTOBER 27, 1960   NO. 22

THURSDAY --- FRIDAY --- SATURDAY

Waterville's Grand Opening

After being inconvenienced for months on end with dust, mud and nearly impassable streets at times, Waterville merchants are officially celebrating the new hard surfaced streets and lighting system in the business district this week end.

It all began late in 1957 when construction on the sewer project started. Work halted during the winter and then continued on through the summer of 1958. In 1959 the streets were given an opportunity to settle. Last spring the city council found ways to finance the much-needed street improvement program. The job is now completed in the business district except for a seal coat, which will be applied next spring.

Waterville merchants are celebrating the new streets and lighting system on Thursday, Friday and Saturday. Stores will be loaded with bargains as merchants welcome their customers in the trade area. The Advance is mailing sample copies of the paper to non-subscribers in the area.

The slogan adopted recently, "Waterville Is On The March", is definitely borne out by the merchants this week. A gala welcome will be awaiting the people of the area and it will be a week end of special prices and bargains and fun. Be sure and read every advertisement.

Remember the days—Thursday, Friday and Saturday.

NEWEST STYLE Remington Portable TYPEWRITERS
REGULAR $79.95
OUR PRICE $49.95
WILCOX PRINTING Waterville, Minn.

$ Free Silver Coin $
In fact we are actually going to pay you to shop at Our Store.
Register for our FREE door prize — No purchase necessary
$ $
SAVE AT JACOBSON'S Farm & Home Supply
Waterville, Minn.

O'Leary's Service
Waterville, Minnesota
EVINRUDE SALES & SERVICE

Schweigerts 3 rings $1.00
BOLOGNA
Fresh GROUND BEEF 2 lbs. 89c
Dusbabek's Market
—We Give Gold Bond Stamps—
WATERVILLE, MINNESOTA

Gambles The Friendly Store
Waterville, Minnesota
END-O-DUST
Main Street Bargains

Marzahn Motor Co.
Waterville, Minnesota

Courtney's
Phone No. 2   Waterville
QUALITY FOOD AT REASONABLE PRICES
WE GIVE EVEREDY COUPONS

Hrdlichka Service & Supply
FRED and IONE HRDLICHKA   Waterville
Phone 121

WEPCO ALUMINUM WINDOWS $11.95
WEBCO ALUMINUM DOORS $43.75
For Your Building Needs Be Sure and Stop At
Central Lumber Co.
Fred Brandt, Manager   Waterville

Deer Hunters INSURANCE
See SCHULZ INSURANCE AGENCY
Walt or Mel

the house that bargains built
Nelson-Wing Fine Furniture
WATERVILLE, MINNESOTA

5-10 BEN FRANKLIN 5-10
LOCALLY OWNED -- NATIONALLY KNOWN
LUTHER'S   Waterville, Minn.

Volkmann Ford Sales
Al Volkmann—owner   Phone 270   Waterville, Minn.

CITIZENS STATE BANK
of Waterville
Member Federal Deposit Insurance Corporation
Friendly, Experienced Banking is a vital ingredient to Community Progress
"We cordially invite your banking business"

Mr. and Mrs. Don Marzahn returned from a ten day trip to New Orleans. (1960)

X

Let's go downtown

Austin J. Murphy
Veterinary Surgeon
Office at P. H. Mulcahey & Sons Livery Stable

DR. E. S. JOHNSON
DENTIST
Office over Greene's store.
Phone 71.
Waterville, Minnesota

M. R. EVERETT
Attorney at Law
WATERVILLE, MINN
Personal attention given to Collections Real Estate and Insurance

GEO. J. DRESSEL
Insurance, Loans, Collections

J. S. LAWLESS
Real Estate, Fire Insurance and Farm Loans.

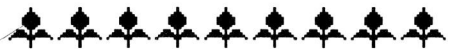

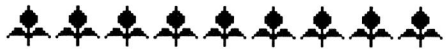

They made a good decision

Before automobiles, towns were located about seven miles apart. This was far enough for a person to travel with a team of horses to do business and still have time to return home before dark. As good an invention as it was, the automobile would eventually lead to closing the doors for many small towns. Waterville would not be one.

The founders of Waterville made an excellent decision to create a city situated between two beautiful lakes. The lakes gave people then and the lakes give people now a reason to come to Waterville for a good time.

This card was sent to a **Miss Laura Stavenau** of Janesville in 1915 from her cousin in Waterville reminding her "to come down once."

Let's go down and see what's happening on the streets of Waterville.

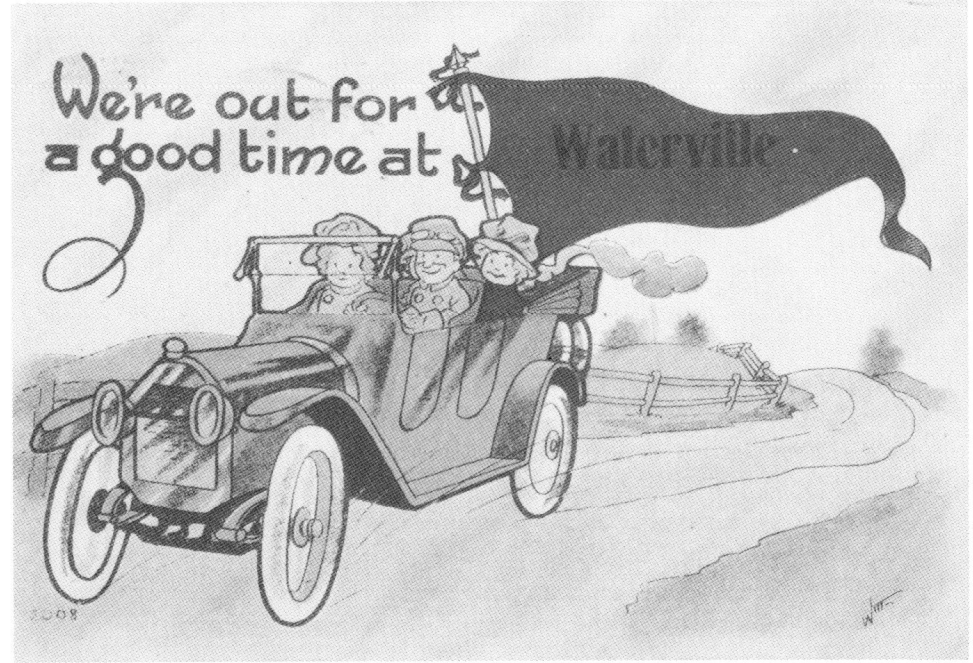

Miss Gertrude Coon and Wencel Feaney were united in marriage at the Catholic Church. June 26, 1914.

 Greetings From Waterville, Minn.

Carved out of the woods

Waterville was less than 50 years old when this photo was taken. By the looks of the trees along the sides of the road, you get the idea that Waterville was carved out of the woods, which it was. Lower Lake Sakatah is only one block from where this photo was taken.

The Security State Bank building is not yet present and will be built across from the **Marzahn** (Leutholds) building.

Those black spots on the road are from some early morning traffic that was headed towards **P.H. Mulcahy** and Son livery stable. The livery stable was in a good location—right next to the City Hall (note the flag pole.)

Although the card says, "Fourth St.," the street today is Second Street.

This card was sent to "Dear Cousin Bertha" in 1908 who lived in Minneapolis.

Business on Main Street

*I*t's Monday morning. **Dr. Cory** has an appointment to get his hair cut at 8:00 before he makes some house calls. He is waiting with **Harry Wendelschafer**. **Harry** is telling **Dr. Cory** about the new garage he recently built.

None of the buildings you see are more than 50 years old. The streets have been recently graded with **Tom Broughton's** wagon. **D. Atherton and Sons** were in town about 6:30 to water the streets. The corners are connected by board walks—a good idea after those rainy days. The Post Office on the north side of the street is open for business. Mr. **William Gish** will take your one cent for a post card. The buildings on the north side (right) are being prepared for a sunny day. All in all, the Waterville merchants are ready for business.

Patrons to the stores will be talking about the recent marriage of **Oscar Finke** to **Bessie Powell**, two of Waterville's well known young people. They exchanged vows on August 12, 1914 at the U.B. parsonage with **Rev. Stone** officiating. The town extends their congratulations and best wishes.

T.J. Slechta wants sewing machines and organs to clean and repair. (1914)

Page 1-2

 **Greetings From Waterville, Minn.**

The sunny side of Main Street

D. **Atherton's** draying service is doing business this sunny, Wednesday, July morning. His rig is parked in front of the post office where he just came from the Dan Patch Electric Line that is east bound to Minneapolis. He has been telling people about the 75 guests the **Andrew Hollinger** family entertained at their home north of town. He was also reminded to tell people to attend the **Frank Hamele's** barn dance this Saturday evening.

Mrs. Frank Pischel sent word from Faribault where she is recovering from an operation for appendicitis. Town doctor, **Dr. Clay**, took her there last week. She will be fine.

Store owners have their awnings drawn on this sunny day. The lady crossing the street has just come from the post office. She is on her way to the Vienna Bakery where **Joseph Miller**, Proprietor, is getting quite a name in town for his special ice cream sodas. After two days of doing the wash, Monday and Tuesday, she felt she deserved a break today.

The door on the far right leads to an upstairs apartment. Years later, those rooms will be occupied by **Dr. LL Rieke**.

Main Street Horseless Carriage

*T*he bank is open for business and doing business. Talk around town is about the new Chalmers "six" car purchased by **C.W. Glotfelter** from **C. W. Christman**. People are wondering how much he borrowed or if he paid cash.

People were also talking about **Louis Gish's** fine touring car that he drove from Minneapolis to visit relatives in Waterville.

It won't be long before all of the hitching posts are gone on Main Street. The gasoline lanterns are being replaced by light bulbs like the one in front of the Security State Bank building.

D. Corcoran warns us that "sugar has gone high but watch our prices, we are always on the job." His store is located to the right of the bank building (north side of the street).

The **F.C. Gibbs** store is in the **F. F. Marzahn** Building on the south side of the street. Leuthold Clothing will soon move in.

Dr. E. S. Johnson, dentist, whose office is located on the second floor of one of the buildings on the north side of the street reminds us that his office will be closed for eleven days while he attends a dental convention and goes on vacation. The little girl on the right in this 1914 card couldn't be happier.

A large bottle of catsup is 19 cents at Edward Liljedahl's store. (1928)

Page 1-3

 Greetings From Waterville, Minn.

Fair worries at Waterville

The year is 1909 and Waterville is buzzing. Another street fair has been scheduled and there is some concern as to how it will go. Parking space on Third Street is already taken. All of the rooms in the Nicollet Hotel above the Ideal Theatre are taken. The YWCA rooms located above the bakery have also been filled.

The Ideal Theatre on the corner of Paquin and Third Streets has brought in some special features. Dubec's comedy circus of dogs, cats, rats, monkeys and apes will be on stage on Friday and again on Saturday evening. The animals are supposed to do everything but talk.

Although it has been an overcast day, talk has it that the skies are clear in the Elysian area.

Waterville has been having street fairs for several years. Some citizens wanted Waterville to bring in the Ringling Brother's circus but the council felt that was beyond its means at this time. Well, it was a disappointment for a lot of children but in 1914 the circus did come to Mankato with its 385 acts, five herds of trick elephants and wrestling kangaroos. Many citizens felt that was close enough.

Lot's of talk on 3rd Street

The couple walking across 3rd Street have just returned from shopping at **L.J. Ebling** and Son store. They felt their price on six Turkish towels for 88 cents was just "outrageous" and commented to each other, "What's this world coming to?" They are going to check out Leuthold's "ten cents off all purchases sale" on Main Street. But first they want to check the billboard at the Gem Theatre operated by **W.D. Haswell** and now showing "Sporting Blood" starring Clark Gable.

The husband wanted to check the action at **Mayland** Billiard Parlor, up the street from the **Ebling** store, but the wife said, "Not this early, you're not. Besides how could you even think of such a thing? We just went to church yesterday."

Waterville is seeing more horseless carriages, not enough to eliminate the hitching posts but enough to warrant a sign at the intersection warning people to "Keep To The Right."

There is a fire hydrant on the corner and if you look closely you can see a newly installed water fountain in front of the post office. Yes, sir, Waterville is booming.

For sale: hunting boats. Contact John Sikle. (1939)

Page 1-4

Greetings From Waterville, Minn.

Business Block on Main Street

It's a quiet day on Main Street. The manager of the Saloon is waiting for his first customer of the day. The Saloon is located in the **George Dressel** building established 1892. The IOOF is up-stairs and **Seidle's** Drugs and Medicine below. There are some rooms to let in the next building and there is a grocery store next to this. The **F.C. Gibbs** store is located in the **F.F. Marzahn** Building.

The boys sitting on the steps and the men on the corner are talking about the most violent wind storm in years that went through on Tuesday evening. **Julius Hiller's** machine shed was blown down. **Otto Ruth** had a horse killed. The tin roof on the south side of the Waterville Furniture Factory was blown off. The rain did about a thousand dollars worth of damage.

P.O' Leary and Sons have bought the milk route from **D. Atheton** and Sons (1914) and the patrons are now being served from the Lakeside farm. **Dennis O'Leary** drives the milk wagon but he will have to avoid the **Lane** and **Lamont** homes that have been quarantined due to smallpox.

Where have all of the horses gone?

Leuthold Clothing Co. has replaced the **F.C. Gibbs** store. The building now contains some of the fanciest display windows in the city. In 1927, about the year of this photo, it offered union suits for girls at 85 cents—while they last.

A pound box of chocolates is on sale for 60 cents at **Didra and Guilbert** druggists (next to **Charlie Quiram's** feed store).

The men on the corner are discussing whether the good spring weather is going to hold through the planting season. Actually, the man on the left is hoping the other will buy him a Fleck's Beer at the saloon located in the building in front of the two Model T's on the right.

S and H Green Stamps are now being offered at **J.J. Dawald's** meat market and at **Edw. Liljedahl's** general merchandise store located on the north side of Main Street.

The horses that used to bring Watervillians to town have been replaced by the horseless carriage. It has been almost a decade since Waterville had three livery barns.

Mrs. Roy Luker (Anna Kanne) was called to rest. Peter Grubish was one of the pallbearers. (1939) Page 1-5

Greetings From Waterville, Minn.

Mailbox Controversy

People are talking about the new Ben Franklin Federated Store that will be built on the corner of 3rd and Main. People are beginning to wonder what will happen to the small businesses when they can offer things for sale at 5 cents and 10 cents?

The post office has installed a mailbox outside the building for the convenience of the customers. Rather than step inside the building to mail their letters, they can just put them in the box located outside. It has been said that there was a suggestion to turn the box the other way so people could just pull up alongside with their autos and mail letters through their car window. Most dismissed the idea as pure foolishness.

The big house next to **Charlie Quiram's** filling station is the home of **Frank Luker** that he purchased in 1945. **Hazel Williams** had a farm behind the station that went all the way to the lake. The store next to the post office is **Sherratt's** Jewelry and **Severson's** grocery. The next store is **Emil Preuss'** Hardware (formerly owned by **Felix Hultgren**). **Emil** is the local agent for the De Laval Cream Separator.

Farmers are in town

The streets are filled with cars and the farmers are in town. Some have come to buy the one and one half pound loaves of bread at the Blue Ribbon Bakery on Third Street at eight cents a loaf. Wives have been complaining that it has been too hot to bake.

Luther's Cash is selling men's ties for 25 cents, women's briefs for hot weather for 49 cents a pair and plain shirts for men for 49 cents. At the National Tea Store next to **Luthers**, **Peter Solyntjes** is selling sugar at 10 pounds for 47 cents.

According to the watch hanging above **Sherratt's** Jewelry on the right it is 9:20 and Waterville is already bustling.

Some of the farm kids may have appointments with **Dr. L.L. Rieke**, dentist (sign on corner of post office) who opened his office in 1933 and is located on the second floor. The wives have an appointment at **Melvera's** Beauty Shop—**Mrs. Melvin Jameson**, proprietor. **Roemhildt's** cafe has a complete dinner for twenty five cents served by cute waitresses.

The city fathers have decided not to enforce the dog license ordinance. (1895)

The phone's ringing

In 1899 the local telephone company was reorganized and named the Cannon Valley Telephone Co. with **J.J. Worlein** as president and **J.A. Carr** as vice president and general manager and **A.J. Kanne** as treasurer.

Audrey Peterson worked as a telephone operator after graduating in 1941 through December 1945. **Irene Lawless** had been there for many years and **Ester (Michaels) Powell** worked nights. **Audrey's** starting wages were 19 cents per hour. **Betty (Aberle) Schwartz, Bernice Smith** and **Irene Van Fleet** worked in the office. The night operator also had to keep the furnace going by adding coal purchased from **Fahnings**.

It was known as the Minnesota Community Telephone Co. **Irene Lawless, Esther (Kritzer) Powell** and **Betty Aberle** were the operators in the 30's and 40's. **Fred Powell** was the lineman.

It's around 1914, people are returning from church and the phones are beginning to ring.

1930's National Food Store

The National Food Store truck is just getting ready to leave after unloading the supplies for **John Sullivan's** National Tea Store located next to **Luther's** Cash store. **Pete Solyntjes**, previous owner, has moved to a new place in the **Rogers'** building (1936). **Mrs. Ernest Chambers** has been waiting for ten pounds of sugar to go on sale at 47 cents.

Preparations are being made for the W.R.C. food sale at **Corcoran's** Cafe located on the left under the big "EAT" sign. After the food sale some of the buyers may want to check out **Guilbert's** Pharmacy (The Rexall Store) across the street where they can buy "Rexall Orderlies" for 25 cents. "Orderlies" are the original chocolate flavored laxative.

You can see the front of the popcorn wagon on the right of the photo. You can buy a bag for 5 cents and eat it while you look in the Leuthold Clothing showcase windows.

L.H. Fuller and L. Towsend broke camp after a six week fishing bout at Horseshoe Lake netted them 1600 pounds. (1891)

 Greetings From Waterville, Minn.

Double parking—our heritage

Notice the cars double parked in front of **Backman** Produce Co. and in front of the **Hasse** building on the left. Double parking was, and still is, part of the Waterville heritage.

Mabel Walz has her beauty shop sign hanging from her house on the left. **Mabel** and **Micky** moved into their house in 1937. **Mabel** opened her shop in 1938. and closed it in 1993 — 58 years is long enough to cut hair. In April of 1943 they bought the **Kanishuer** house better known as **Dr. Cory's** house and office.

Gus Hinz had a shoe repair store located next to the **Hasse** building. The **August Messal** family would move there later and also have a shoe repair business.

Dr. Chris Rohrer and **Lydia** will open an office in the **Haase** Building in 1930 and during their first month in Waterville, he will make $5.00. The **Tom Suchomel** and **Burda** dry goods and groceries store located in the New **Hasse** Building has one pound of Atwood coffee for 25 cents. Phone 47 if you are interested—and, yes, they do have free delivery.

Waterville's Diner

Next to the Cities Service was **Harold's** Lunch. It sold sandwiches, soft drinks, candy, cheese, eggs, and cigars. **Harold Lilysdahl** and his mother ran the diner. It was later run by **Fritz** and **Audrey Taylor**. **Jeannette Morris** says she has fond memories of going to her dad's (**George Hagel**) station to get some money to buy a hamburger from the old Minneapolis and St. Paul street car—Waterville's diner.

This 1940's photo was taken from **Axel Anderson's** oil station on the corner of 1st St. and Main. Next to the diner is **Art Roeglin's** repair shop. On the far corner is the **Bliss** Hardware (later **Mel Jacobson's** Hardware) that had a dance floor upstairs.

George Hagel owned the station in the late 40's. At one time he had an undercover agent working for him by the name of Mr. Lubbers. He was keeping an eye on the Commercial Hotel where a few bank robbers allegedly were staying. **George** was a volunteer fireman, helped with civil defense and was a mayor of Waterville. In parades he would dress up like a clown and drive a 1914 Model T Ford.

Jenanne Pope, Jeanette Stempl, Gladys Preuss, and George Miller are on the school honor roll. (1944)

Page 1-8

 Greetings From Waterville, Minn.

Display at Dusbabeks

Pete Solyntjes is now giving away S & H Green Stamps at his store (**Pete's** Food Market) located on the west side of 3rd Street. On the way down you might stop in for a cold one at **George Wendelschafer's** Waterville Liquor Store also located on the west side of the street. He has Fleck's Beer on tap.

It's a September day in the 1940's and Waterville is seeing a little business. **Harold Mack** Motors (later **Johnstons**) has some nice new Chevys on display. **Dusbabek's** Market has a display of many articles recently received from **Robert** who is in the Navy in the Pacific. The Pepsi truck has stopped at the Bowling alley to get ready for tonight's action. **John Nelson** has a new line of sofas.

People are talking about the unfortunate accident that **Joe Kapaun** had while duck hunting with **Harold** and **Herb Bemis** and **Hiller Teff**. Somehow, he lost his thumb.

George Hagel, mayor, issued a proclamation that the city of Waterville refrain from all sales of intoxicating liquors on V-Day. "Let us make V-Day a day of thanksgiving and prayer," says **Mayor Hagel**.

A pound bag of prunes—25 cents

The Commercial Hotel has burned and **Earl Bliss's** popcorn stand has replaced it. **Mildred Clark** has moved into the office once used by **Dr. Rohrer** and operates a beauty parlor.

A boy (**Dennis**) was born to **Ruth and Ray Kalow**. Ray works at the Security State Bank at the corner of Main and 2nd.

A girl was born to **Mr. and Mrs. George Backman**. **George's** dad, **Charles**, owns **Backman's** Produce.

In checking the *Want Ads* in 1946 (about the date of this photo), **Mrs. Edgar Eggers** has a child's two-piece, all wool light blue snow suit, size 3 for sale. It was worn very little. (It must have been mine. I never did like wool—too scratchy.) Call her at 14 if you're interested.

Wouldn't you know it? There's a car double parked in front of **Dudley's** Red Owl Store on the left. They must have been after those one pound bag of prunes **John** had on sale for 25 cents. **John** managed the store in 1943 after **Tom Suchomel** and utilized the entire store in 1950. He added on the store in 1960 when he and his brother, **Vince**, managed it.

Citizens are reminded to mail Christmas packages for the soldiers overseas by October 15. (1944)

 Greetings From Waterville, Minn.

Your friendly banker

It's around 1937 and my father, **Edgar Eggers**, has just begun his banking career at the First National Bank located next to the Our Own Hardware store on the right. In 1941 the bank would change its name to Citizen's State Bank. My father would retire 36 years later. My father knew what it meant to be a successful banker in the 40's, 50's, 60's and 70's. It meant knowing the citizens and taking an interest in them and in the community. He knew the needs of the farmers and he recognized that the citizens of Waterville wanted a banker they could trust, respect—someone with a high degree of integrity. That's my father.

Before working at the bank, my father worked at **T. J. Suchomel's** grocery located up the street in the **Haase** building.

Bob Buckmaster managed the hardware store after **Emil Preuss** and later **Al Werner** would manage it.

Leo Anderson has just taken over the management of **Anderson** Service Station and will sell Skelly Gas (corner of Main and 1st Street).

Oily streets and band concerts

Before the hard surfaced streets, downtown streets were frequently oiled to keep the dust down. The mixture of oil and tar made quite a mess. The woman walking across the street to the post office is going to complain to postmaster **Al Koelzer**.

She has an appointment to see **Walt** or **Mel Schulz** about some car insurance. Their office is located in the basement near the drug store on the left. Waterville Motor Company is advertising '54 Fords for sale for as little as $10 per week.

Congratulations are in order for **Julaine Roemhildt**. She is the Valedictorian for the graduating class of 1954. **Mary Ann Walz, Marilyn Lorenz, Nancy Schwichtenberg** and **Kenneth Weilage** will sing solos at the baccalaureate and graduation ceremonies. The procession will be led by **Dorothy Ann Balfe**.

Waterville residents are looking forward to the band concert to be held next Wednesday, June 9, under the direction of **Harold Hebl**. The concert will be in the band shell located in White Water Creek Park on north 3rd Street.

Dr. Holtan has just notified the citizens that they are to clean their cesspools, sheds and barns. (1939) **Page 1-10**

 **Greetings From Waterville, Minn.**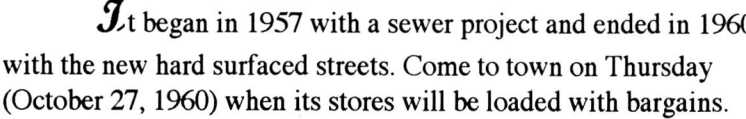

Waterville Is On The March

It began in 1957 with a sewer project and ended in 1960 with the new hard surfaced streets. Come to town on Thursday (October 27, 1960) when its stores will be loaded with bargains.

Waterville's latest enterprise was the opening of **Simes** Bowling Center. **Don** and **Bonnie Simes** announced that league play started Monday. A picture in the *Advance* showed all lanes filled with **Dale Campbell** about to pick up his ball.

Waterville dumped New Richland on Wednesday with sophomore, **Dean Taylor**, scoring all four touchdowns. **Mark Sheehy** finished 12th in a regional cross country meet. **Al Volkmann** wants everyone to stop in and see the 1961 Falcons. **Richard Wong's** O.K. Cafe has a noon lunch special for 65 cents. **Glenn Preuss, Art Roeglin** and **Kenneth Kletschka** left Friday to do some pheasant hunting in South Dakota. **John** and **Vince Dudley** are selling ground beef at 39 cents a pound at the newly remodeled Red Owl.

How do you like the new litter bins installed by **John Schmidt** and **Don Coon**? "Welcome To Waterville" signs and new litter bins—Waterville marches into the sixties.

Lazy day on south 3rd Street

Well it has been a few years since **Joe Styer** had a shoe repair shop in that first stucco building on the left. The **Eldo Reed** Family and the **Don O'Brien** family would live there some day.

It's a quiet lazy summer day in Waterville in the 50's. Now is the time for Watervillians to go "up north." **Mr. and Mrs. Al Fredell** and **Demaris** and **Tim** left Tuesday for Cohasset to spend a few days at the **Harold Bemis** resort.

Leon Mager, son **Leon, Jr.** and **Donald Solyntjes** left on Tuesday morning for Lake Bemidji. **Leon** filled up his car at the Webb station located north on 3rd Street for 30.9 cents per gallon.

George Greer left a note on his door of the **George Greer** Auto Company saying that he would return in ten minutes. He went over to **Marlowe Burns** Cleaning across the street. **George's** business at 3rd and Paquin features new Chryslers.

Fahning Supply Company is on the right. **Harold Preuss** who has his office on the second floor will gladly sit down with you to look at some house plans. It looks like Waterville business people will do a lot of sitting today.

John Frodl and Hugo Antl were chosen as directors of Waterville Coop. Creamery. (1952)

 Greetings From Waterville, Minn.

Get your chains ready

Stan Blowers built the building on the right and just as the **Bob Mills** buildings left their mark on Waterville in the early 1900's, the **Blower's** buildings do the same.

It's in the mid-sixties and the **Fahning's** lumber yard is still standing in the same spot where it was standing sixty years ago. They have, however, exchanged the coal business for home insulation.

As you drive north on 3rd Street you won't see **Zollner's** Feed Mill. It has been gone for a couple of decades. A car wash built by **Willie Beer** has replaced the Webb Gas Station. A flag is flying over city hall that is now in the old telephone building and a Speed Wash is located in the Gem.

The face of Waterville continues to change. Thirty five years ago **Mack** Motor Company up on the right was advising people to stop in and get tire chains before the heavy snow. We should be glad there is one constant in Waterville—the weather. It will always be there.

Closed for the day. Gone hunting.

You won't find **Eddie Eggers** and **Glenn Preuss** downtown this morning. If you drive south to **Vern Hans'** slough you may find them there or you may find them on the northeast shore of Mud Lake. **Glenn Preuss** probably put a sign on his bake shop on this day in 1944 that said, "Gone hunting." The ducks were flying today. My dad is 27 years old and there are about 35 ducks nailed on the board.

"Gone fishing," or "gone hunting" signs were found on the doors of Waterville businesses now and then and why not? If there is a difference between the Watervilles of today and the Watervilles of yesterday it is in the way people spent their time, they knew their priorities—church, home, duck slough.

Shirley Fessel has completed her beauty school course. (1961)

Greetings from Waterville, Minn.

Waterville Landmarks:
Many are gone, some remain but aren't the same

The Waterville VFW WWII Honor Roll of Heroes

Sergeant *Arthur Schultz* was reported missing in action some time ago and recently his parents (**Mr. and Mrs. Richard Schultz**) were notified that he was a prisoner of war in Germany. As the ball turret gunner of a Flying Fortress, his duties were to protect the "underbelly" of his aircraft. Many Nazi fighters have felt the sting of the turret's twin machine guns as it slowly turns in constant readiness. *(Advance)*

It was for people like **Arthur Schultz** that this billboard was intended. **Donald Preuss, Ken Grover, Clarence Kaupa, Robert Dusbabek, John Raedeke, June Dehn, John S. Backman, Harry Stowe, Mason Lamont** . . . Some are still with us, many are gone—but never forgotten.

There are differing views as to where this billboard was located. Do you know?

Gary Coon, son of Mr. and Mrs. Howard Coon, was home on a furlough. (1959)

Greetings from Waterville, Minn.

Dr. Osborn's Minkery

I wrote a letter to **Seth Osborn** before he died in 1994 thanking him for this card. I told him that for a boy in 1950 **Osborn's** mink farm was one of Waterville's most exciting places. It was the next best thing to having our own zoo. On more than one occasion my brother and I went with **Bob Rausch** to catch an escaped mink. **Seth** said that at one time it was the largest mink ranch west of the Mississippi. It employed 50 men and had a monthly payroll of $2,500.00

    Dr. S.S. Osborn was a veterinarian in town for many years. His wife, **Mildred**, one of Waterville's hall of fame bridge players, lived west of **Osborn's** dam in a cottage. Each morning **Dr. Osborn** would get a shave from **Walt Schulz** for 15 cents.

    The mink business in Waterville supported many families. **Howard Anderson** operated a sizeable mink farm on the southwest side of town as did **William Quast**. (Call 231 if you have disabled horses to sell to **William**.)

Invest in Waterville furniture

Here's a believe it or not story for you. Several years ago I purchased a pile of boards at a garage sale in Bemidji. While putting them together, I discovered they were the parts to an antique secretary. Not so interesting? On the back of the secretary was a label — "Made in Waterville, Minn., Waterville Furniture Factory." Now that's kind of interesting.

    The **John Babcock** Furniture Factory was built in the middle 1850's. The original building burnt down in the 1870's and **L.Z. Rogers** rebuilt it. The company sold china closets, buffets, library tables, piano benches and pedestals. Their 1916-1917 catalog contained 38 pages. An oak china closet was priced from $11 to $18.00. An oak buffet was $14 to $34.

    The secretary stands in my home office and will remain standing long after you and I are gone. "Furniture for a lifetime, Waterville, Minnesota."

We never pay less than $15.00, even if the horse is unable to get up. Osborn Mink Farm (1952)

 **Greetings from Waterville, Minn.**

Gem Theatre: Dreams became real.

Roy Rogers was starring in "Rough Riders Roundup." My brother **Craig, Roland Bittrich** and I made the beautiful "Gem" theatre our second home almost every Friday night in the late 40's and early 50's. Manager, **Mr. Cameron**, dressed in a dark suit and tie, was always present to take our nine cent ticket (babies were free).

The girl in the picture is **Nancy Dusbabek Minks**, sister to **Bob Dusbabek** and daughter of **Frank** and **Clara Dusbabek**. **Nancy** says she was walking toward her dad's store when the photographer asked her to stand in front of the theatre. She later found the postcard on sale at **Luther's** 5 and 10.

S.H. Farrington opened the first motion picture theatre in 1912 on the second floor of the **Jacobson** Hardware store. The Gem was built in 1942 by **William Haswell** and he sold it to **Mr. Cameron** in 1948. **Mr. Cameron** sold it to **Cub Simpson** where it eventually became a furniture store operated by his son **Don**. My brother saw the last movie in the beautiful Gem (*Farewell to Arms*). There were four people in attendance. The Gem: The End.

Technology comes to Waterville

It was the telephone operators job to turn on the siren when there was a fire. Then the whole board would light up with people wanting to know where the fire was.

"Number Please?" How many times did **Arlene Schwartz** and the other Waterville operators say that in a day? Our number was "14." What was yours?

Irene Lawless was a long time operator. **Dr. Cleveland Cram** informed me that she took a personal interest in the customers. He remembers calling his mother who was not at home, "but **Irene** had heard her talking with my aunt about going to the movies that evening so **Irene** called the owner of the Gem Theatre and he called my mother out of the movie to take my call."

Waterville converted to dial phones on December 4, 1961. The city was expected to purchase the phone company building and convert it to a library. Other operators besides **Arlene Schwartz** were **Mae Hoban Kritzer, Dorothy Solyntjes Mager, Mrs. Hazel Cleveland, Mrs. Fred Poehler, Mrs. Gilbert Luker, Mrs. Ken Murker,** and **Mrs. Pearl Lauer.**

Waterville Oil Company, Jim Balfe, proprietor—dial "1."

Greetings from Waterville, Minn.

Waterville's Wal-Mart

Mammoth Department Store, Waterville, Minn.

The Mammoth Department Store was founded by **L.Z. Rogers** before the turn of the century. The date and name are still on the building (Rogers: 1857-1891). The first date refers to an earlier building that was destroyed by fire. The second date is the date the now standing building was built. **George E. Greene** became a clerk in the store after he graduated from the Waterville Schools in the late 1800's. Both the **Greene** family and the **Rogers** family were very important to Waterville's early history.

George's father, **William**, helped organize the first bank in town in the late 1800's. It was located in the middle of the block on the west side of Third Street. In 1904, **George Greene** followed in his father's footsteps and assisted in the organization of the First National Bank later to become Citizens State. **Rogers** served the county as a state representative and later as a senator. He was an intimate friend of Governor Hubbard.

The O.K. Cafe was more than OK

There were five teen "hangouts" in the fifties - the O.K. Cafe, **Larson's** Cafe, Red Top Cafe, and **Courtney's** Cafe. If only those booths could talk! But it was the fifth teen hangout that was the most popular — Woodtick Hollow south of the Narrows.

J.J. Dawald's Butcher shop was originally in the OK Cafe location.

The **Richard Wong** family managed the cafe during the 50's. They were very well liked in town. **Richard** always wore a smile and was always polite. His young son, **Eddie**, would often sit on the front steps. I suppose he grew tired of people asking him, "Hi, **Eddie**, what's wong?"

THE MOST POPULAR PLACE IN TOWN
O.K. CAFE - GOOD FOOD
WHERE TOURISTS STOP AT WATERVILLE, MINN.

Earl E. Greene, fireman, USN, is serving aboard the destroyer USS Henley. (1952)

Greetings from Waterville, Minn.

The Waterville Water Works: everyone's security blanket

The Waterville water tower was and always will be a welcome sight for Waterville residents. It's probably the one landmark we take for granted—it doesn't get a whole lot of respect. But it has been there for many years and like a lighthouse welcoming ships into their home port, the Waterville water tower reminds us of the importance of having some things remain the same in our lives.

The railroad tracks running east and west belong to the Chicago Great Western railroad. The smokestack to the right of the tower was part of the system that helped push the water up the tower. It has a capacity of 17,000 gallons.

This photo was taken in the first two decades of the 1900's.

Marzahn Building: 100 in 1995

The **F. Marzahn** building was built in 1895. The name and date are forever embossed on the building as is the **George J. Dressel** building that was built in 1892. Both buildings are shown on this card. Sandwiched between the buildings is the Odd Fellows or I.O.O.F. building. The **F.C. Gibbs** mercantile store occupies the Marzahn building and a tavern occupies the **Dressel** building. **R. R. Riley** occupied the store before **Gibbs**. A drug store is in the I.O.O.F. building. **Anton Stucky** will open a drug store (Rexall) farther up the block in 1935.

Today these buildings are occupied by Potential Unlimited (formerly Leutholds), The **Dean Thrun** Agency (formerly **Comstocks** Market) and Coast to Coast formerly owned by **H.H. Hunte** and then **Ben** and **Ann Kniefel**.

George Dressel and Art Scheid went to Glencoe to attend the funeral for Attorney Merrill. (1939)

Greetings from Waterville, Minn.

Wanted: People to de-tassel

Not too many youth in Waterville escaped without detasseling corn. Northrup, King provided many youth pocket money for pulling the tops off of corn during hot summer days.

A full page ad in the 1957 *Advance* read, "Men and women of all ages are needed. No previous experience is necessary. No limit on individual earnings. Often whole families work together, detasseling 20 or more acres, and earning $300, $350, $400 or more in three week s." (phone 8 if you are interested).

Adjacent to Northrup, King was a stock yard. **Cleve Cram** was a stock buyer for the local farmer's association. He sorted stock and held them in pens until the Minneapolis and St. Louis freight train came. As many as six car loads of livestock daily were shipped out during the 1920's through the 1940's. **Dr. Cleveland Cram**, son of **Cleve** said, "I was a boy of about 14 then and had to help out, so I remember how hot it was on a summer night loading all that livestock—and smelly, too. But life was hard but good in those days and everyone worked."

Luther's Ben Franklin Store

In the second store window at the right are posters advertising the need for people to buy war bonds. In the second store window from the left are pictures of Waterville soldiers fighting in World War II.

William F. Luther, son of store owner **Bill Luther**, was a veteran of World War II and, no doubt, he was serving at the time this photo was taken in the early 1940's. The names of the people in this photo are identified in another photo found on page 9-7.

Bill Luther was a long time resident of Waterville. His son, **Jack**, eventually took over the store. My father, **Eddie**, served as their bookkeeper for many years. At one time, **Jack** hired me to wash every florescent light in the building after the new streets were put in during the early sixties.

Just as the Waterville Mammoth store of the early 1900's provided everything needed for Waterville residents under one roof, **Luther's** did the same in the 30's and later. It was Waterville's Mega Mall—everything for 5 and 10 cents.

Mr. Joseph Webber, aged 81, passed away at the home of Ed Hamele. (1909)

Greetings from Waterville, Minn.

Yes, Waterville had a hospital

As you look at the hill on the north side of lower Sakatah, imagine a large Victorian style building. No, it's not a home but a hospital. You are visiting the Samaritan Home (used for recovery) to check in on **Mrs. Marzahn** who just gave birth to **Mason**. There are two "Guardian Angels" pictures over her bed.

The Good Samaritan House and hospital were built in 1873 for a **Dr. E. P. Case**. (**Ken Mader** and **Bill Olson** currently live on this land that also belonged to the **Allen Wilcox** family.) **Hazel Allen's** mother, **Fannie Robbins,** worked there. The hospital burned in the early 1900's. After the fire, **Dr. Case** used the Tetonka Hotel to house his patients.

A **Dr. C.P. Dolan, Dr. George Chamberlain** and A **Dr. LL Moench** practiced medicine in Waterville prior to 1916. **Dr. W.M. Cory** was another pioneer doctor of Waterville and was still practicing medicine in 1916.

It's too bad about those "Guardian Angel" pictures. Not to worry, **Mary Lou Solyntjes** has them hanging safely in her home.

Security State Bank

"Behind us lie 3 &1/2 years of deadly struggle in which, with God's help, we have prevailed. So, today, we celebrate a victory." This was an ad in the September 5, 1945 *Advance* sponsored by the Security State Bank at the close of the war.

C.W. Glotfelter was the bank president in 1908 and **F.J. Hinze** was the cashier. In 1914 the bank had capital of $25,000.

A note in a 1939 *Advance* said that **Ray W. Kalow** spent last Thursday in St. Paul on business. **Ray** was an employee in the bank before moving to Nerstrand to direct a bank in that city.

Note the barber shop sign and pole. **Harold Dressel** inherited the law practice from his father and had an office in the back. For a time their practice was called, **Dressel** and **Dressel**.

Ernest "Snub" Nahlovsky's barber shop was in the basement of this building. His specialty was flat tops.

Built in 1908, the top floor served as a Masonic Hall. Thanks to my father and **Arnie Leen** who purchased the building in the 70's, (and later sold it) the building remains in excellent condition.

Art Quiram is the owner of a new set of harness purchased at Bill Kalow's Harness and Shoe shop. (1930)

Page 2-7

 Greetings from Waterville, Minn.

Waseca roughnecks at Maplewood

Waterville's second and last Chautauqua came to a close on Monday evening with a less than enthusiastic audience. The Waterville *Sentinel* of 1914 reported that "this is to be regretted by all who love good clean, high class entertainment."

While in town, many of the Chautauqua performers stayed at the Waterville House and took advantage of the boats at the boat livery located on the south shore of Lake Sakatah.

Some of them rented boats to attend the local dance at Maplewood Park on Lake Tetonka. Their enjoyable time was marred by a few roughnecks from Waseca. Attending the dance was **George Andrus, Bill Atherton, Bill Quast** and **Oscar Finke** who just returned from Sparta, Wisconsin where they were encamped with their militia company. The roughnecks were no match for our young soldiers.

Ole Kin will not be using a boat so often, as he just purchased a fine new Buick "six."

The Beach: Where the action is

The swimming beach always had some action and most kids hung out at the beach during those hot summer months. On one occasion I dove off of the dock and hit the bottom with my head and cracked my front tooth. When **Dr. Rieke** saw it he didn't seem to be too alarmed. It is still cracked.

Tom Enquist announced that the final public band concert will be given on pontoon boats to be held at the Waterville Beach—weather permitting. Bring your lawn chairs or take your boat out. Show time is at 7:00, August, 1960.

The Waterville Sportsman club is conducting a fund drive to take care of the algae in the lake. A few of the many people that have donated are: **Ray Bremer, Jack Backman, Dick Childs, E.J. Petricka, Bill Warburton, Mrs. Wulff, Leon Nesbitt** and **Merlyn Matz.**

After the concert people will be heading out to the grand opening of the A & W Root Beer Drive-In located at the junction of Highways 13 and 60.

Don Bohn is honored at the State Fair. (1961)

 **Greetings from Waterville, Minn.**

Waterville's CCC Camp

The Civilian Conservation Corps camp was located on the **Perry Pope** and **Del Pope** property north of Lake Sakatah. It was built around 1935. **John Frei** was the first camp commander. Local girls were disappointed to see it dismantled in 1940.

The camp was home to some Waterville boys and many other boys from the Dakotas and Kansas. A few of the boys married local girls. Do you know any?

Thanks to the camp crew the dam across the Cannon River near **Osborns** was constructed in 1937. The CCC camps helped bring the U.S. out of the great depression. It was one government project that worked.

A few of the boys will be on the local boxing card to be held at the high school gym that has been rented by **L.J. Bruns.**

John O'Leary's station

As you entered the side door and looked to your right, there would be a nice selection of guns. Not only did **John** sell guns, for young boys, you could find anything else you needed at **O'Leary's** station. My brother, **Gene Preuss** and I would make a trip a day to **O'Leary's** just to look at his selection of fishing lures, buy a pop or an ice cream and talk to **John** about fishing. **John** was always Mr. Congeniality and still is today.

John fixed my father's Evinrude, sold us minnows and always mixed in friendly conversation. At one time **John** had a nickel that was bolted to the floor but you didn't realize it until you tried to pick it up, which, of course, was impossible to do. I thought that was a pretty neat trick.

Not much has changed since John took over the business from **Robert Rosenau** in March of 1943. This photo could have been taken 30 years ago but, in fact, it was taken in 1996. To me **John O'Leary's** station is one of Waterville's most sacred landmarks.

Ida Lyons, Carrie Corcoran, Irene Courtney, Cathy Giles, Cora Stockton, and Irene Robson attended the Eastern Star convention in St. Paul. (1939)

 Greetings from Waterville, Minn.

Let's ride the CGW

That's **Miss Marie Haie** rushing to catch the Chicago Great Western train that is going to Mankato. She will be visiting friends there. The year is 1914. The CGW Depot sat near the water tower that you can see in the background.

Some of the guests that attended the recent marriage of **Adolph Fritz** and **Miss Emma Berg** came by way of the CGW.

It's time to plant cucumbers. The Waterville Pickle Co. is offering free seed if you need some.

Economic news around town is that **Mr. E.S. Giles** is closing out his stock of groceries and intends to retire from business. **Thomas Slechta** is contemplating opening a moving picture theatre in the **Giles** building where **Stanglers** is now located and **Arnie Norman's** grocery prior to them.

Mrs. Ernest Herring wished she would have been on the CGW the other day when she broke her limb by jumping out of a moving buggy.

The Commercial House Hotel— and playground

It was one of the best hotels in Southern Minnesota. Suspected bank robbers would even stay there on occasion. You know they have good taste.

H.G. Schulz built it before the turn of the century. He owned and operated it for over fifty years. It was located where **Dudley's** Red Owl had their parking lot at the corner of Main and Second Streets.

On a cold winter day in the early 1940's it burned to the ground. It's cement basement became Waterville's first downtown playground directed by the **Walz** sisters.

Speaking of **Schulz** families, **Walt Schulz**, local barber and insurance agent, was the father to **Melvin Schulz** who married **Eva Stucky** whose mother, **Dora**, sold shoes for **Kalow's** Harness shop on Third Street as well as worked at **Luthers**. **Mel** was **John's Dudley's** first carry-out boy.

Harry Greer has sold his residence in Morristown and will move to Waterville. (1946)

Page 2-10

Greetings from Waterville, Minn.

The Waterville Bridges: places to drive to, drive on, fish from, jump from and hide under

The Reed Street White Water Creek Bridge: A bridge of dubious distinction

Jack Backman wrote on the reverse side of this card, "I smoked my first corn cob pipe under this bridge—got real sick and couldn't answer call to dinner."

The **Charles Backman** (**Jack's** father) house was located just north of this bridge on the west side of the road. It was later purchased by **Dr. Dunnwald**—a long time Waterville veterinarian. It still stands.

White Water Creek was an excellent creek for spring time northern spearing as most boys could attest to who lived in West Waterville. We would usually start at the bridge and work our way north and east. I don't recall anyone ever getting any but the thrill of the hunt surpassed the agony of our wet feet and muddy pants.

The bridge was built by the Faribault Paving Company in the second decade of the 1900's.

Ezra Wolters is having the time of his life starting a fur farm. He has 13 fine coon and 16 mink. (1929)

Greetings from Waterville, Minn.

"Dear Ralph, I was in swimming yesterday. You ought to be here."

The Cannon River represented the "old swimming hole" to many people. In this photo, it looks like it was just a hot day and someone said, "Let's go swimming." "Hey Mom, we're going swimming down to the old swimming hole." And they did.

L.Z. Rogers had more than a swimming hole in mind when, as secretary of the Cannon River Improvement Company in 1865 and while he was serving in the Minnesota House of Representatives, he dreamed that some day the Cannon River would be a gateway to the Mississippi. He was Waterville's first real dreamer but the railroad killed any notion he had of establishing a water route to the Mississippi.

This 1918 photo was taken where the Cannon River flows into Lake Tetonka—near the **Roy Raedeke** addition. You can see the lake in the background. (sent to Master **Ralph Ebert** in Iowa City on July 29, 1918)

A good bullhead spot

This place was and still is a pretty good fishing hole for bullheads. As you are driving on the north side of Lake Tetonka on County Road 12 and cross the Cannon River bridge, look south.

According to **Mary Lou Solyntjes** as told by **Hazel Luker**, it has been said that as Faribault trappers were going up a river they had a small cannon in their boat or canoe. They tipped over and lost the cannon. From then on it was christened the "Cannon River." Now you know the rest of the story.

Thomas Sikel has completed and delivered to Wallace Brown ten new boats. (1945)

Greetings from Waterville, Minn.

One of Waterville's first entertainment centers

When this Tetonka Drive bridge was placed across the outlet to Lake Tetonka in the early 1900's, it opened one of Waterville's most popular entertainment centers. There's something about bridges that causes people to stop, stand and stare into the water. Well, many people have done just that over the years and they continue to do it today.

Picture a September moon reflecting on the shimmering Lake Tetonka waters. There's a slight ripple in the water and as you drive over the bridge, you see the silhouettes of a half dozen or so fishermen. One of them is **Marlowe Burns**. **Marlowe** knows all about taking walleyes in the vicinity of this Lake Tetonka Boulevard Bridge. He's a charter member in Waterville's Hall of Fame of outstanding fishermen and can tell you how to catch walleyes in Lake Tetonka—and how to get your clothes dry cleaned.

Next time, stop and take a look. There's always something to see.

Do you suppose the four mallards swimming below the bridge are related to the mallards that swim under the bridge today? How many people do you see in the photo? I count four.

The Lake Tetonka Boulevard Bridge was built in 1905 and ever since people have been fishing from it. It was quite a novelty to have this new fishing spot for Watervillians. It was still a novelty fifty years later when the local fish hatchery would put a fish trap below the bridge to catch the carp and buffalo. There would be standing room only for onlookers. When **Roland Ruths** and his fish hatchery buddies would take the carp from the trap, it was better than watching a professional wrestling match. All of that thrashing and splashing and escaping—well, you just had to be there.

(Note: On the left side of the photo and on the opposite side of the lake, notice all of the trees. Lake Tetonka has the appearance of a northern Minnesota lake—rugged and untamed.)

Thressa Bittrich passed away at the age of 92. (1957)

Page 3-3

Greetings from Waterville, Minn.

"Let's go down to the dam."

The above phrase became part of every Watervillian's vocabulary when **Osborn's** dam was put in by the CCC in 1937. When the lake was too windy for boats or when you just wanted to go fishing without the fuss and bother of having to take a boat, people went to the dam. There was always action at the dam. **Clarence Harriman** and I would even take our dates to the dam — just to stop and take a look. How romantic!

In this photo you see exactly what the dam did to improve the recreational attractions in Waterville. There are kids fishing from a raft on the far side of the river, about a dozen cars are in **Osborn's** lot, some people just came to look, and both men and women are fishing.

Glenn Preuss recently caught some 43 silver bass in less than an hour. Word about catching fish spreads fast in a small town and these people are hoping to duplicate **Glenn's** luck. **Glenn** would be the first to tell them, good fishing isn't luck.

Hey, that's me!

Nothing has changed. It has been twenty years since the dam was built. A new bridge has replaced the old wooden bridge on Tetonka Boulevard located beyond the dam. Kids have become a little more daring. Now they are sitting on the dam bridge railing. But what hasn't changed is that the dam is still attracting people.

This photo was taken in the summer of 1953. I should know because I'm the ten year old kid with both hands on the railing third from the left. On my right is **Dennis Bittrich** and **Gretchen Rausch**. **Gene Preuss** is the kid with the straw blond hair third from my left and that's **Jennifer Rausch** sitting on the railing.

The greatest dam fisherman wasn't actually a man at all. It was **Lena Eggert** who was also a good friend to all of the kids who fished at the dam. She used no fancy Shakespeare reel or rod. Her cane pole was adequate enough to catch all the sunfish one ever needed — and she did.

Norman Preuss is assigned to the air base in Japan as a baker. (1952)

Greetings from Waterville, Minn.

Watch out for trains!

As you travel up stream from the **Osborn** dam bridge, you would eventually travel under this railroad bridge that ran north and south. **Tom Broughton** may have owned the farm in the background. This card is dated 1909.

Every time I walked across this bridge as a youth, I could imagine myself getting a foot or leg caught in the open trestle followed by the sound of an oncoming train.

Why was Waterville built on the south side of the lakes?

When you traveled to Waterville from the north, you had to cross this bridge and when you left Waterville from the south to go north, you had to cross this bridge. One of the side boards on the bridge reads, "Waterville Livery - Finest Rigs In The City." Do you see the man on the bridge with the bicycle watching the man in the boat? **John O'Leary's** Conoco station will eventually be built to the left.

How did the early settlers who came from the south get across the river? Maybe they didn't bother and said, "This spot looks good. Let's stop here. Someday others will come and stop here too."

Alfred Miller would occupy a cement building on the north side of the bridge. He would ride a bicycle, sleep in a hammock and attend church on Christmas Eve.

The new Lutheran parochial school of St. Peter's Church at Cannonville was dedicated. Professor William Christjaener is in charge of the school. (1914) Page 3-5

Greetings from Waterville, Minn.

The Lake Sakatah Bridge— Waterville's Golden Gate

I often wondered if there were any regrets among Watervillians when the bridge was put in to separate lower Sakatah from Upper Sakatah. I suppose the people on the north side were glad that the main traffic entering and leaving Waterville would not have to pass by their homes. And then I suppose there were some business people who were upset that Highway 13 would no longer pass directly through Waterville. Nevertheless, all would have to admit that the 1950's bridge did give visitors a feeling that they were entering a community that enjoyed showing off its lakes—and that's what the bridge did.

It's 1957 and one person who we will not see crossing this bridge is **W.B. Cameron,** manager of the GEM. He accepted a position as manager of the Chief Theatre in Red Wing. His son, **Robert**, will remain in Waterville for the time being.

Traveling on the old road

This card was sent to **Sarah Townsend** from her sister in 1907. She wrote, "When far apart remember this is the old road we have often traveled." How many times have you taken a trip to "the Narrows Bridge" on the old road?

News from the "Narrows" in the *Sentinel* of May 1, 1914: "**Frank Hamele** had the saw mill at his place last week and sawed the lumber for his new barn." **Frank Hamele** is the grandfather of **Bernadine (O'Leary) Hildebrant**. **Theresa Hamele, Frank's** daughter, married **John O'Leary.**

The Narrow's Bridge was built in 1905. According to the writings of **Jim Hruska,** an Indian named **Cut Nose** ran a ferry at the Narrows before the building of the bridge. He owned a farm by Horseshoe Lake and lost the farm for a sack of flour and a rug. He was hung at Mankato because of his involvement in the Indian Uprising of 1862. Abraham Lincoln signed the document ordering the hanging of the thirty-eight Indians. Cut Nose was buried and then dug up to be studied by Dr. Mayo of LeSueur.

Miss Tresse Hamele visited the Narrows school Friday. (1914)

Greetings from Waterville, Minn.

Waiting to see the train pass

*I*t hasn't been too long since this trestle bridge was built over the Cannon River that separates Sakatah from Tetonka. The man in the boat is waiting for the Minneapolis St. Louis train to pass. When the photographer asked him why, he said, "Just to look at it."

The man had good reason to take a look because just a few days ago (August of 1914), the train derailed just north of Main Street. He will be one of many people from Waterville who will be taking the train to the State Fair for $2.80.

Once the train passes he is going downtown to see the large tarantula that was captured yesterday afternoon in **Bliss'** grocery store. It was found by **Mrs. E.H. Willman** in a bunch of bananas. **Mr. Bliss** has bananas on sale for the rest of the week.

The house you see in the background at the corner of Marion and First Street is still standing today.

For further information address any of the following progressive business firms.

The Waterville Sentinel
Commercial Hotel
New Gem Theatre, W. L. Buck, Mgr.
Security State Bank
J. E. Seidle, Druggist
J. S. Lawless, Real Estate
Hultgren & Schwickert, Hardware
H. W. Wendelschafer, Garage
Sherratt & Son, Jewelers
C. H. Bliss, Groceries & Hardware

Julius Kapaun
Progress Cash Store
Chas. Darche, Groceries
Joseph Miller,
Vienna Restaurant
Central Lumber Co.
Otto Meyer,
"Health Office" Saloon
Jungers & Johnson,
Garage
W. J. Kalow, Harness
Lorenz Hansen,
Blacksmith

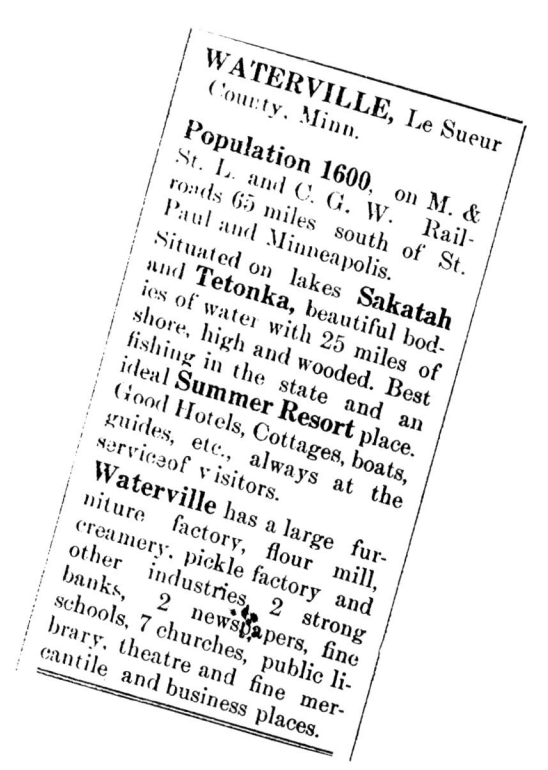

WATERVILLE, Le Sueur County, Minn.
Population 1600, on M. & St. L. and C. G. W. Railroads 65 miles south of St. Paul and Minneapolis. Situated on lakes **Sakatah** and **Tetonka,** beautiful bodies of water with 25 miles of shore, high and wooded. Best fishing in the state and an ideal **Summer Resort** place. Good Hotels, Cottages, boats, guides, etc., always at the service of visitors. **Waterville** has a large furniture factory, flour mill, creamery, pickle factory and other industries, 2 strong banks, 2 newspapers, fine schools, 7 churches, public library, theatre and fine mercantile and business places.

Alexander Marble had over 100 spring chickens stolen one night last week. (1885)

Page 3-7

Greetings From Waterville, Minn.

Fire, floods, fairs and other significant Waterville events

Wreck on the M. & St. L. Ry at Waterville, Minn.

Head-on train collision in Waterville.

Can you imagine the excitement a train wreck would bring to a small town? You can also imagine the talk in the local taverns and barber shops. "Did you see the wreck? I tell you I never saw such a sight in all my life. They say the engineer was sleeping on the job."

The date of this photo is in the early 1900's. The train wreck occurred in the **Emil Hruska** pasture where the highway 60 bridge crossed the Minneapolis and St. Louis track.

Don O'brien, Diane Moench, Nelda Lamont, and Roger Knish graduate from WHS. (1952)

Greetings From Waterville, Minn.

Wreck brings booming business for Waterville merchants

People are beginning to come to view a sight that not many people have seen before. A lot of questions will be asked. "How can two trains headed towards each other be on the same track at the same time?" "How will they ever get the cars back on the tracks?" "Did anyone bring any sandwiches?"

Some of the merchants in town probably wish the wreck would stay there for awhile. Business is going to be booming in the next few days with writers and railroad workers and, not to mention, the sightseers from Elysian, Kilkenny, Waseca, and Morristown who will come to town to see up-close their first real train wreck.

Some will come and look on their way to **Ben Quast's** auction on the 16th of September of 1914. **W.J. Hancuh** is the auctioneer. **Ben** will be selling eight good milk cows and five spring pigs. The event will be held on the **Kading** farm on Cannon River five miles northwest of Waterville.

Now you kids stay away from there!

Not likely. People like to see the unusual. In a small town where the usual happens most of the time, the unusual is bound to pique a person's curiosity.

This is October and school is in session. Teachers will probably be having their students write some themes about the wreck. Some topics come to mind that teachers might ask their students: "The advantages and disadvantages of rail transportation." "Why the covered wagon wasn't such a bad idea after all." "If you were the engineer, what would be your thoughts?" "If you should go near the wreck and get hurt, what would your father do and/or say to you?"

What to write was, no doubt, on the minds of **Harold Dressel** and **Clarence O'Leary** as they left town by train to attend Creighton University in September of 1914.

Little Richard Allen was injured by a log rolling on him at the Gish saw mill. (1946)

Page 4-2

Greetings From Waterville, Minn.

Two men die in a strange place

Headlines in the *Sentinel* in July of 1914 read, "Freight train wrecked one mile south of Waterville Tuesday morning and two men killed." The two men were "beating" their way to the Dakota harvest fields and were from Indiana. Both lay together under two cars of coal. The bodies were placed in the charge of **Worlein** by coroner **Otto L. Marx**. The coffins were shipped to Indiana and were covered with beautiful flowers placed there by the people of Waterville who were deeply touched by the tragic end of the young men in a strange place.

The postcard shows another wreck that occurred in April of 1910. It's a different wreck than shown in the previous two photos because the front of the engine is not damaged. It is, however, another Minneapolis and St. Louis train.

People are getting used to train wrecks in Waterville. The conversation now around Waterville is, "Oh, by the way, did you hear about the train wreck outside of town?" "No, I can't say that I have. Are the fish biting anyplace?"

Let's clear the tracks

I'm still wondering what happened to the scrap iron. I suppose if you were to dig along the tracks, you might find some remaining steel from this train wreck.

This wreck happened north of town and the photo is looking south. You can faintly see the Waterville water tower to the left on the horizon. On the right you can see the steeple of the Episcopal Church.

I'm sure the old timers pictured here must have had a good time going out to the wreck and then visiting one of Waterville's many taverns to talk about what they saw.

"Yeah, they just hauled a bunch of new ties to fix the track."

"You don't say?"

"Yeah, that's right. I just come from there."

Talk like this kept Waterville humming for the next six months.

George Hagel and family have moved into their home recently purchased from W.J. Kalow. (1939)

Page 4-3

Greetings From Waterville, Minn.

Maria: Handstand Expert

"Ladies and gentlemen. Step right up and witness one of the most daring, death defying, never performed feats of all time. The marvelous Maria will balance with one hand while the stool spins around faster than you can say 'Meet me in Morristown.' Drum roll, please"

This photo was taken by **Christman** but when he developed it, it was developed backwards. That's why you can't read any of the writing. It is taken across from **Corcorans** on Main Street.

The card was addressed to **Mr. Walter Ebert** of Waterville sent from **Ellen Fritz** of Waterville on January 8, 1909.

Oh, yes. Maria was seen performing the same, "never before performed trick," the following day in Medford.

This was a white shirt and tie event for the men and boys and ladies wore their best hats. **Chris** and **Louie Ruedy** were there. The **Bill Cram** family was present and **Elmer Smith** and his family. Yes, it was a special day in Waterville in October in 1908. Aren't you happy for them that it wasn't raining?

Benito, Flying Trapeze Artist

At the top of this photo you will see Benito the clown
hanging upside down.
Benito made a bet
that he would need no net;
the Waterville crowd appreciated his act without flaws
so they gave him a standing applause.

The people of Waterville have been talking about this street fair for many months. To think that a real carnival was coming to the streets of Waterville in 1908. Oh, there was the usual talk that it would attract some riff-raff and rumors were going around town that some youth had decided to leave with the carnival folk when they left and, "Was your son one of them?"

This photo was taken in front of **Joseph Miller's** Vienna Bakery. There is a "Made to Fit" shop across the street. This is the site of the later to be Red Top Cafe where teens like **Paul Prahl, Florence Quiram** and **Joan Fonken** would gather in the fifties. Farther up the street on the right is the **Dr. A.V. Barnett** veterinary surgeon building.

Cpl. Ralph Vail received his honorable discharge from service. (1945)

Greetings From Waterville, Minn.

Street Fair A Great Success

Waterville's 4th annual street fair, which was held the last three days of last week, was a great success in every way. There was a good street parade with some fine floats and decorated cars both Friday and Saturday mornings. There were dances at the Auditorium on the first two nights and there were special attractions at both Ideal and Gem theaters during the fair.

That was the news in the October 2, 1914 *Waterville Sentinel*.

Fred Zollner won first prize for the best decorated auto. **Frank Luker** won first prize for the best apples. **Herman Neindorf** for the best squash; **Mrs. P. Feany** for the best cabbage; **Mr. Emil Antl** for the best watermelon; and **Ernest Dehn** for the best pumpkin.

Waterville vs. Elysian

In 1914 the friendly rivalry between Waterville and Elysian had already established itself. The *Sentinel* reports, "The tug of war on Saturday between Waterville and Elysian was a hard pull but the home men proved their superiority."

The tug of war and street parade took place on Main Street. **I.G. Kin** has a tavern in the location where **Luther's** store will be located. A Flicks Beer sign hangs in front of the store. A barber shop is located to the east of the tavern.

When a big event like the fair happens, it does precipitate other events that are less welcome reports the *Sentinel*. "It seems there was 'one nuisance that should not be tolerated.' This nuisance is confetti. How any fun is to be derived from littering the streets and people's hair and clothing with this stuff is more than we can see. Further more, confetti is pie for the rowdies who feel at liberty to throw it in the face of any woman or girl they meet."

There you have it. And to think it all started with confetti.

Gus Stavenau of Chehalis was transacting business in town Monday. (1914)

Page 4-5

Greetings From Waterville, Minn.

Commercial Hotel Fire

January 2, 1947, the day of the Commercial Hotel fire, is a day many Waterville residents still remember.

The Commercial Hotel was situated on the old **Dudley's** Red Owl parking lot. It offered overnight lodging as well as long term lodging. The hotel was owned by **Bill Liably**.

Don't you wonder where the people who were residents in the hotel stayed the next day—people like **Sylvia and Art Roeglin**?

Mickey Walz tended the bar the night it burned. **Nellie Cribbs (Spooner)** had the restaurant where The Main St. Lounge is now. She opened up her cafe and made coffee for the firemen.

One man, **Iza Marple**, and two dogs, "Stormy" and "Lady" died in the fire. Stormy was a big St. Bernard dog.

Firefighters Fighting Fire

Donna and Mary Ann Walz, Joe and Melvin **Studnicka** were among the kids that roller skated on the vacant cement basement foundation of the Commercial Hotel for a number of years until the hole was filled. **Mabel Walz** still has a few relics from the fire.

Howard Anderson rang the alarm to alert the firemen. He says he also helped remove the liquor from the building but people were taking it as fast as he could bring it out so he gave up.

Bill and **Martha Krings** owned the hotel before **Liably**. **Martha** was known for her great pies. No doubt the pie crust was made with butter.

On a very cold morning after the fire, my mother pulled my brother and me in a wagon from southwest Waterville to see the hotel. It was still smoldering. To this day, people still talk about the Commercial Hotel fire.

Joan Ruths was inducted into Beta Gamma Chapter at Mankato State. (1966)

Greetings From Waterville, Minn.

Decoration Day, 1914

Decoration Day or Memorial Day has always been a special day for Waterville. I remember marching with the scout troops down to the stone bridge on Hoosac and 3rd Street. The VFW would have a gun salute while the scouts and parade goers threw flowers in the White Water Creek.

The order for this 1914 Memorial Day parade was: Waterville Cornet Band, N.B. Barron Post, Women's Relief Corps, Ladies of the G.A.R., Mayor and City Council, Board of Education, Board of Health, Waterville Fire Department, Civic Societies, **Professor Woolverton** and Teachers and pupils of Waterville Public Schools. The clergy and citizens were cordially invited to join the procession.

Businesses were encouraged to close from 2 until 4 in honor of the nation's dead defenders.

Snowblowers needed

Without snowblowers snow removal was a real problem for Waterville businesses. Merchants like **Dave Corcoran** whose "3 Store System" was located on this Main Street block. **J.J. Worlein**, **C.H. Bliss** grocery store, **Joseph Miller** bakery, **J.E. Seidel** of Waterville's reliable drug store and **R.R. Riley** of The People's Store would need to get to their stores early to remove the snow before their customers would begin to arrive.

Notice the band stand at the end of the block? There won't be need for that for a few more months.

Ed Courtney would eventually manage **Corcorans**. It seems it was kind of traditional for **Ed** to cross over the street to **Luthers** and have **Dora Stucky** help him do his Christmas shopping at 6:00 on Christmas Eve.

This photo was also taken in the early 1900's. "The Fair" store is located at the end of the block about in the place where **Sherratt's** jewelry store was located.

Mrs. Jake Grobe is visiting with her daughter, Mrs. Roy Jewison of Lake Elysian. (1914)

Greetings From Waterville, Minn.

Floods hurt area business

You are looking at the Tetonka Boulevard bridge at the turn of the century. Heavy rains and high water left over from the spring thaw have resulted in another flood for Waterville. People like **F.C. Gibbs** were out in their buggies inspecting the damage. Attorney **Dullam** was thinking he might start selling flood insurance but people thought it was a ridiculous idea.

The flood hasn't helped business any. **Ed Young** hoped to get on the road to sell organs for **P.H. Martin** but not with roads the way they were. **Mrs. Kettlewell** had put in a new stock of millinery but no one would be in to look at it.

Road to north side

Charlie Quiram, in the middle wagon, is making his morning delivery to the north side. **Charlie** worked for **Ernie Giles** grocery that was located where **Stanglers** is located. He shouts to **Roy Hopkins** who is fishing from the sidewalk, "Hey, **Roy**, If I see any road kill fish, you can have 'em."

This is another early 1900's photo that depicts the road to the north side, or in those days, Minnesota 13. This road was the main thoroughfare to Waterville and much busier when travelers had to compete with schools of carp and fishermen.

John O'Leary will eventually have his station and cabins farther up the road on the right. The Cannon River bridge is also farther up the road. Rumor has it that Roy caught a big carp and put it under Ernie's wagon seat.

Fong Moon opened a laundry. (1909)

Page 4-8

Greetings From Waterville, Minn.

A funny way to fight the flood

Forget the flood. Let's fish! Men, women, children, boats, nets, and flood water. The flooding of Waterville's rivers has always resulted in some interesting activities by its citizens. This First Street scene separating Tetonka from Sakatah and leading to the north side saw much activity on this spring day.

To the left, women are fishing, boys have their pants rolled up, and men are seining while being watched by boaters. One seiner is even wearing a necktie so you know he's serious.

It's early in the spring around the turn of the century and gardeners were hoping to get their cucumbers and cabbage planted for the J.S. Gedney pickle factory in town. Haley's comet was coming on the scene and people like **W.H. Miner**, **Keyes Swift** and **Clarence Kanne** felt this to be a good omen for gardening.

Flood of September 2, 1906

Floods are nothing new to Waterville. The person rowing the boat is on Third Street in front of the **Fahning** Lampert's Lumber Yard. The building to the south of Lamperts is a hotel. I don't know which one. It's either the Minnesota Hotel or the Waterville House Hotel.

The sign in the middle of the road says, "Look out the cars." This sign could have been a prank because three years later **C.W. Christman** (the person who took this photo) would sell a Ford touring car to **Ira Hotellan**. This would make the fourth automobile in town. I doubt if Watervillians were even thinking of looking out for cars in 1906. A more appropriate sign would read, "Look out for carp."

George Pond and game warden Polzin liberated 45 English pheasants in the timber near Elysian. (1919)

Page 4-9

Greetings From Waterville, Minn.

Irene is in a parade

That's **Mr.** and **Mrs. Frank West** in the buggy ready for another Waterville Street Fair. **Irene Corcoran**, sitting between the two, was looking forward to this day. It's not every day that you can be in a parade.

You can see the old Advance building located on Third Street where the Lake Region Life office is now located. The Waterville Cigar Factory sat on the corner of Main Street and Third Street.

The family of **Joseph Stangler** was wishing he would have been with them as they watched the parade. It was about one year ago (1911) that one of Waterville's oldest citizens died.

Horses don't require batteries

The girls in the front auto in this 1913 street fair are **Margaret Hieftelem**, two **Kempton** girls and **Dorothy Marzahn**. The parade is going west on Main Street. Cars are still considered to be an oddity and people have come from the surrounding communities to see them. They are still considered to be noisy and expensive. Farmer **G.W. Bluhm** says his horses don't need a battery and I have a whole field full of fuel.

The Piper building or cigar factory is located where **Luthers** will be. That would be the fourth building on the right. The bandstand is located directly opposite it on the north side..

Some people in town were sorry to see the Tetonka Hotel move to Montgomery. It seems a **Dr. Havel** purchased it and was going to use parts of it to build a hotel in that community. In days gone by visitors would stay at the hotel and come in to town to see the parade. The hotel was located on the north side of Lake Tetonka.

Mason Marzahn's large truck was destroyed by fire at the A. Schmidt farm. (1945)

Page 4-10

Greetings From Waterville, Minn.

"Keep the altar fires burning."
The churches of Waterville

In 1957 the pastors of the Waterville area churches were:

United Brethren Church - Stanley V. Propp
First Baptist Church - Francis Grubbs
Holy Trinity Catholic - James MacCormac
Lakeside Methodist - Joseph H. Grostephan
North Waseca Lutheran - Charles Akre
St. Andrews's Episcopal - Douglas Pitts
St. Peter's Lutheran (Bell) - H. W. Mueller
St. Paul's Lutheran - Henry Maye
St. John's Lutheran (Kilkenny) - E. M. Kuerschuer
Trinity Lutheran - H.F. Eggers

Apparently religious leaders felt that the Waterville area could support ten churches for one of two reasons: One, we were a city of sinners and two, business would be good. In both cases they were right. You could and still can count on the altar fires to be brightly burning in Waterville.

Rector, T.R. Park will deliver a sermon entitled "Modern Tithe" at the 11:00 service at St. Andrew's. (1960)

Greetings From Waterville, Minn.

I know that guy

Who's the handsome guy pictured in this photo? How surprised do you think I was when I found this post card in Iowa with my grandfather, **Rev. H.F. Eggers**, pictured on it?

Trinity Lutheran Church was organized on January 31, 1909 by **Rev. C. Albrecht** from St. Peter's Lutheran Church (Bell). At the time of the organization, services were held at the United Methodist and the United Brethren Church. Services were held in the **John Fahning** house before this time.

In 1919 **Rev. Winter** was installed as the first resident pastor. The Trinity Lutheran Ladies Aid organized in 1923 with **Mrs. W. Christjaener** as president.

Mrs. Grace Fahning was the first confirmant in German in 1913. The first confirmants in English were **John** and **Paul Fahning** in 1915.

Rev. H.F. Eggers was installed on January 17, 1926. When my grandfather retired in 1957, **Pastor Victor Roth** succeeded him. **Pastor Erwin Meitz, Jr.** is the current pastor and **Rev. Karl Eckhoff** is pastor of St. Peter (Bell) Lutheran.

Trinity Lutheran Parsonage

There he is again. Photographer, **Ryan**, probably caught my grandfather walking over to the church (He always dressed for work. Seldom did I see him without a tie.). "Pastor, how about being in my picture of the church?"

My grandfather probably responded, "Ah, they don't want to see me."

My dad, **Edgar**, maintained the gardens located between the church and the parsonage. The apple trees are just beginning to grow near the parsonage. The trees and the porch swing provided many hours of pleasure for me and my cousins **Dennis** and **Gary Kalow, Jean, Karen** and **Tom Krause, Joyce, Peter,** and **Scott MacMillan**.

The cornerstone was laid for the church on October 12, 1924. Members of the Building Committee were **Wm. Christjaener, Otto Roeglin, Julius Preuss,** and **F.G. Quiram**. The cost was $11,000. The parsonage was built at a cost of $5000 in 1926.

"Wanted: Servants of God" is the title of Pastor B.F. Koch's sermon, pastor of United Methodist. (1944)

Greetings From Waterville, Minn.

Some of my best friends are Catholic

The ground breaking for this new addition took place on May 13, 1957. The cost of the new addition was $60,000.

In some communities you could tell who was a Catholic or a Lutheran by the kind of car they drove. Lutherans drove Chevy's and Catholics drove Fords. As a Lutheran, we weren't taught that Catholics were necessarily bad, you just didn't want to be caught alone with one for any length of time. Lutherans never could figure out what making the sign of the cross meant. Obviously it was some sort of secret code used to signal there were Lutherans watching and that they might break out in song at any minute.

As it turned out Catholic and Lutheran kids tended to ignore the teachings of their parents. Some of my best friends are Catholic.

Indian Ponies and Father Dolan

When **James Timpane** arrived in Waterville in 1855, he was the first and only Catholic among the early area pioneers. He was joined in 1856 by five more Catholic families. The first Catholic priest known to have visited Waterville was the **Rev. Father Ravo** in 1857. In 1867, more Catholic families arrived: **Dennis O'Leary, John** and **Pat Murphy, Slechtas, Mariskas, Lallas,** and **William O'Leary.**

Rev. Father Keller came once a month to the farm house of **Patrick Dolan** (the **Patrick Dolan** farm is where **Ken Slechta** now lives). According to an article in *Lake Region Life*, **Father Keller** would leave Faribault on a Monday morning with a number of Indian ponies and in an open buggy drive to the **Dolans** then proceed to visit other churches in the area. He would return to Faribault near the end of the week.

Before 1881 worship services for Waterville Catholics had been held only occasionally. In 1882, **Father Christy** from Waseca came to Waterville and organized the parish and secured the site where the church now stands. It was built in 1884.

Rev. Roth will be having communion announcements at Trinity Lutheran from 3-5 and 7-8 P.M. (1961)

Page 5-3

Greetings From Waterville, Minn.

Father Lucey—1st resident priest

In 1892 **Father Lucey** came to Waterville as the first resident priest. The parish house was completed that same year. The property for the church and the parish was obtained from **Rachel Harn** and husband in 1879.

The first parish rosters include the names of **Timpane, McGovern, Burke, Hans, Cavanaugh, Lawless, O'Brien, Mariska, Stangler, Weaver, Dawald, Dusbabek, Wesley, Brophy, Slechta, Lallas, Groh, O'Leary, Murphy, Frodl**, and others.

The arrival of Father Mac

The cornerstone for the new parish church was laid in 1952 under the direction of **Father James MacCormac**. The new parish house was completed on December 23, 1969, under the supervision of **Father Mark Farrell**. **Father James MacCormac** came to Waterville in 1946.

Father Mac administered the last rites to **Mary E. Grubish** in April of 1952. **Herman Nuendorf, Clarence Prehn, Romeo Watzek, Peter Solyntjes, A.J. Koelzer,** and **Frank Knish** acted as pallbearers.

Mary was born on March 2, 1875 at Waterville, Minnesota. She was the daughter of **Charles** and **Mary Slechta** and graduated from the Waterville Public Schools in 1894. She married **Peter Grubish** on October 20, 1897 in Holy Trinity. The **Rev. Dennis Sullivan** officiated at the ceremony.

Father Michael Ince currently serves Holy Trinity Catholic Church.

Holy Trinity Catholic: James MacCormac, pastor; Masses at 7:00 and 9:00 A.M. (1956)

Greetings From Waterville, Minn.

Grotto, Waterville, Minn.

ST. ANDREW'S EPISCOPAL
Douglas Pitts, Rector
9:30 a. m. Church school.
11:00 a. m. Morning prayer and sermon.

NORTH WASECA LUTHERAN CHURCH
Charles Akre, Pastor
Sunday morning service at 9:30.
Sunday school at 10:30 a. m.

TRINITY LUTHERAN CHURCH
H. F. Eggers, Pastor
Church services at 8:00 and 10:00 a. m.
Sunday school at 9:00 a. m.
Trinity Lutheran Women's Society will meet Thursday afternoon at 2:30 at the home of Mr. and Mrs. Walter Meinke.
Bible Institute at St. Paul's Lutheran church, Waseca on Monday, November 18th, at 8:00 p. m.

What about the grotto

One of the mysteries of Waterville for me was "The Grotto." An early issue of the *Advance* stated that the "Sheridan Corner was recently purchased and the grounds beautified by an outdoor shrine, of three parts, in memory of the pioneer priests and people of the parish." This was in honor of the church's Golden Jubilee Celebration held in 1929 for their 50th anniversary. **Father John Volz** was priest at the time.

Always on the job, in the 1860's **Father Ireland** (later Archbishop) was visiting Waterville and stopped at the Sheridan's blacksmith shop located east of the Gem Theatre, to have his buggy repaired. While he was waiting, he was able to round up a few Catholics and baptize some children.

Between the years 1879 and 1880, occasional services were held. In 1881 a society was organized, a dwelling house purchased and remodeled as a church.

Joan Ruths, Janet Frodl, Mary Prenzlow, Joanne Roessler and **Mary Roemhildt** probably missed a few church services in June of 1957 when they attended a Seven County 4-H camp at Camp Patterson, on Lake Washington.

Catholic Church, Waterville, Minn.

Sally Otoupal has been employed as manager's clerk at the Glacier Park Hotel in Montana. (1957)

Greetings From Waterville, Minn.

The first wedding: Mary Frodl and Frank Pittman

Mrs. **Mary Frodl Pittman** passed away on January 20, 1944. **Rev. James MacCormac** officiated at the service. Pall bearers were her grandsons **James Pitttman, Norbert Mariska, Francis Pettepiece, John Roessler, Jr., Leonard Maas** and **Gordon Randall.**

Mary Frodl was born in Austria on May 7, 1865. She came to America with her parents, **Mr.** and **Mrs. Frank Frodl** when she was two years of age. In 1883 she was united in marriage to **Frank Pittman** at Holy Trinity Catholic Church. It was the first marriage in this church. **Frank** was killed in a cyclone at Morristown in 1900.

St. Andrew's Episcopal Church: The oldest building in Waterville

"The friendly white church on the hill" was begun in 1870 and completed in 1874. Can you picture **Bishop Henry Whipple** consecrating the church on a bright, sunny day in July of 1874 with the pride of its members radiating from their faces? And, they had a right to be proud as the first established church in Waterville to hold services. It is Waterville's oldest building.

In 1919, the year of this photo, the rector of the church was **Rev. Neil E. Stanley**. And, yes, the church has always been white as a 1985 sand blasting of its old paint revealed many layers of white covering its honey-gold pine boards. Next time you pass the Episcopal Church, bow your head in reverence to "The friendly white church on the hill."

The oldest hotel in Waterville was the Waterville House established by John Dawald in the 1870's.

Greetings From Waterville, Minn.

Who was the first minister of the Episcopal Church?

Organized in 1858. **Rev. J. Lloyd Beach** was the first minister. **Lewis Stowe** and others formed this church, but the organization was not really perfected until 1870 when sixteen members constituted the church.

A church edifice was started in 1870 and completed in 1874. In 1882 **Reverend E.G. Hunter** was the rector and the parish contained twenty-six members. In 1916 the church owned a full block in West Waterville.

Herman Solyntjes remembers putting the cross on top of the steeple after it was cleaned with the help of the Waterville Fire Department and **Fred Hrdlicka.**

The **Rev. Josette Martins** now serves as the Priest of St. Andrew's Episcopal Church.

First Baptist Church

It began on September 2, 1860. Eight believers met with **Rev. E.S. Smith** at Waterville school. Charter members of First Baptist Church were: **Zoan Rogers, Seth H. Kenney, David Temple, L.Z. Rogers, Mary E. P. Smith, Phoebe Rogers, Julia F. Rogers, Helen S. Rogers, Mary E. Sheldon-Miner**. On September 16, 1860 these charter members organized the First Baptist church. In 1882, the present building was constructed without the aid of a pastor for $3000.

At first the church was seated with chairs and later with opera seats. The church was remodeled in 1913 and a basement was placed beneath it.

E.A. Witte now serves as Pastor at First Baptist Church.

Rev. Douglas Pitts celebrated Holy Communion at 8:00 at St. Andrews Church.(1959)

German Methodist Church

It was in the year 1866 that Waterville Methodist Episcopal Church was organized in Morristown, Minn. by **I.H. Richardson**, pastor at Morristown. The new congregation had a membership of about 20 persons. **C.P. Blair, A. Tidball, William Green, Charles Church** and **Z. Rogers** were duly appointed trustees.

The other side of this card says, "German Methodist Church, later used by beginning Trinity Lutheran, later the residence of **Paul Pomeranze**."

Mason Marzahn, Dr. Rieke, Mrs. Frank Luker, Mrs. Ted Lyons, Eldo Reed

The first year of the 20th Century found 93 members in the Waterville Church, with 150 enrolled in Sunday School. A salary of $700 was paid to the Pastor.

1916 began the 12 year pastorate of **James Castles**, who is remembered by many and who was apparently one of the outstanding pastors of the conference at the time. He served the ministry until 1928 and retired in Waterville.

The construction of a new church began in 1953. The name "Lakeside Methodist Church" was chosen for the new church. The building committee was **M. Marzahn, Dr. Rieke, Eldo Reed, Mrs. Frank Luker, Mrs. Ted Lyons**. **Harold Preuss** drew up the plans.

Ozro Baldwin, manager of Baldwin's resort died at the age of 63. Services will be at the United Brethren Church. (1959)

Greetings From Waterville, Minn.

Lakeside Meth Church - Waterville, Minn.

George Blaie donates plan

Rev. Grostephan was pastor of the First Methodist Church at Waterville when it was organized in 1865 and in 1916 had a membership of 65.

The same year a church building was erected, the first in the community. The land was donated for the church and parsonage by **George Blair**. Owing to a shortage of funds the structure was not fully completed until 1870. It was built almost solely by the hands of **"Father" Radin** and **William Greene**, who went into the woods and cut the timbers for the building. Some of the early pastors were: **Reverends T. McCleary, W. Satterlee, George W. Richardson**, 1866-1867; **Levi Gleason, E. Bowdish, G. Way, L. Tower, E. Hawley, Jabez Blackhurst, John Lowe, A. Butt.**

The current pastor at Evangelical United Methodist Church is **Rev. Mark Schneider.**

The U.B. Church

I will always remember the old United Bretheran Church for one special reason. I was never in it when it was a church but when it became the **Wayne Prosch** Funeral Home, my grandmother's (**Alma Raedeke**) wake was held there. She died at the age of 100 in 1988.

The U.B. Church was a familiar site to the residents in West Waterville. It stood right on the corner and when you went up the hill going north, a stop sign awaited you. If it happened to be slippery, it was hard to get going again. On the other hand it was great for going down the hill in the winter on a sled.

The church was located on the corner of Herbert and Main Streets. Through the efforts of **V.A. Cook** the only United Brethren Church in LeSueur County was started in 1893. The charter members were **Mrs. A.C. Davis, Glenna Davis, Mr.** and **Mrs. Lukes, Doctor** and **Mrs. Umphrey, Mr.** and **Mrs. Broadbent, J.D. Buell** and **Eugene Rugbee**. The church building was started in the spring of 1891 and completed and dedicated in 1893. It would eventually merge with the Methodist church.

CHRISTMAS
— CANDLELIGHT SERVICE —
Sunday, December 24
10:30 — 11:30 A. M.

Christmas Message:—
"'Twas the Night before Christmas"

UNITED BRETHREN CHURCH
Rev. O. E. Brunelle, Pastor

Everyone Welcome

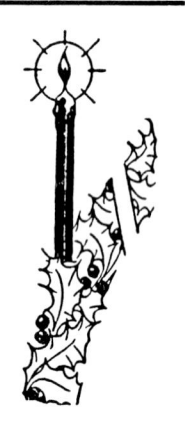

Funeral services for Ed Courtney were held at Lakeside Methodist in November of 1957. He was 56.

Greetings From Waterville, Minn.

"Our business men are all of the up-to-date, courteous kind and all handle large stocks of goods"

*W*aterville, LeSueur County, is one of the best small towns to be found in Minnesota. Our business men are all of the up-to-date, courteous kind and all handle large stocks of goods. We have in our midst the following factories: a fine pickle factory; a large furniture factory which ships its output all over the United States; planing mill; one of the greatest plants for the making of Amber Cane Syrup which is pure; one fine machine shop; and grain elevator. Our schools are rated second to none in Minnesota. We have eight churches and fourteen lodges. The present population of Waterville is about 1,400 and we are rapidly increasing. The farming country surrounding us is of the best. All farmers in our locality are becoming wealthy. Our district is noted as one of the best in the state for raising stock and is the best dairy country to be found anywhere. (Waterville Commercial Club, 1913)

It's interesting that the Commercial Club overlooked the lakes and what's in them in their marketing description of Waterville. But maybe 1913 was one of those years when the fish didn't bite. This photo of walleye and bass, all caught in Lake Tetonka, was taken in 1914 or 15.

Stop in at J.J. Dawald's meat market for the best in home-killed beef. (1916)

Page 6-1

Greetings From Waterville, Minn.

Down Town At The Commercial Hotel

As you came into Waterville from the north, the Commercial Hotel was the first hotel you saw. It was right down town, had a nice porch and had good food. If you came to Waterville in the early 1900's during the summer, you passed the popular Maplewood Park Pavilion (late **Doc's** Silver Streak Pavilion) where **Slechta's** orchestra was playing.

People passing through probably said, "Let's spend the night here and come back for the dance." They stopped at the Commercial Hotel, had some supper and drove back to the dance.

The hotel was owned by **H.G. Schulz** (the grandfather of **Paul Schulz**) at the time. He built and operated the hotel for over fifty years. It burned to the ground in 1947 when it was owned by **Bill Liably**.

Casserole for supper

This card is a little tattered and torn—kind of like the way the owners of the stores in this 1918 scene felt after a day at the office. A great cure was to go home and find a tunafish or hamburger casserole waiting for them. If you were to walk the Waterville streets in the second decade of the 20th Century, you would find **Jenkins** Central Lumber, **Jim Traver's** Commander Elevator, **R.R. Riley's** People's Store, **H.E. Peterson's** Jeweler, **Jos. Miller's** Vienna Bakery, **S.W. Van Guilder's** Livery, **J.E. Seidle's** Drug Store, **Ruedy Bros'** Dry Goods, **Lawless** Real Estate and others.

It's now 1996 and you will find **Berg's** Pharmacy, **J.C. Ryan's**, **Robert Oser**, **Krazt** Massage, **Thrun** Insurance, **Jerry Apple** Auto Parts, **Prosch-Dennis** Funeral Home, **Mark Bemis** Well Drilling, **Chambers** Construction, **Tom Knish** Plumbing, **Ray Volkman** Electric, **Veen's** Super Value, **Denny's** Bar, **Lowell Renken's** Phil Mart, **Dave's** Mobil and others. A lot has changed but these same people still go home to a tunafish casserole.

The Gem Theatre is being redecorated according to the owner Mr. Haswell. (1935)

Greetings From Waterville, Minn.

Street Maintenance In The '30's

Waterville is preparing for its tourist traffic. **Tom Broughton,** Street Commissioner, is busy these days. **Vince Hancuh** (on the right) is ready to get to work so he can have some time to go after those crappies biting in Lake Tetonka.

Tom uses a grating system with a team of horses to smooth out Waterville's potholes and washboard roads. He also has a horse drawn street sprinkler wagon to use on city streets so people like **Mrs. Glotfelter, Mrs. E.M. Lawless, Mrs. Armitage** and **Mrs. Charles Christman** don't have the opportunity to complain about Waterville's dusty streets. I gather, however, that **Tom** was a pretty conscientious and kind man and did his job to the best of his ability. People realized that it was difficult to be a good Street Commissioner.

The Leuthold Clothing Co.

In 1900 fur coats were $6.00 at Leutholds. I purchased a suit at Leuthold Clothier in 1976 for my 15th year high school reunion for about $100.00. They were having a going out of business sale.

In 1895 **F.F. Marzahn, Dr. C.P. Dolan** and **D.B. Parsons** erected the brick block building at the corner of Main and Second streets. In 1896 **James Quirk** and **George Gardner** erected a brick block building at the corner of Paquin and Third Streets (this occupied the vacant lot north of the old Gem Theatre). The Leuthold Clothing Company occupied the corner building managed by **Adolph Oppliger** who was followed by **Elmer Armitage**. They later moved to the **Giles** building on Main Street (now Potential Unlimited).

My dad was always impressed with the quality of clothes sold at Leutholds. He must have been right because I still have the suit I purchased in 1976. It pays to shop in your home town.

Capt. John Raedeke returned to Germany after a 15 day furlough, His new duties will be under Gen. Eisenhower. (1945)   **Page 6-3**

Luthers: For men too!

The stock of **Luther's** Store was moved to the new building on the corner of Main and Third in August of 1940. **Luther's** was originally on the north side of Main Street.

It was a real family store. You could buy anything for the kids, for mom and even for dad as announced in a 1932 ad. In 1932 **Luther's** Cash Store advertised that "This is a men's store too!" In the same ad they advertised razors for 10 cents, work socks 10 cents, fancy suspenders 50 cents., leather belts 50 cents.

The year 1952 was a special year for me. I went into **Luther's** to buy my school supplies and walked out with a box of Crayola crayons—the box of 48—the big box. That was the year I got mostly "A's." With a box of 48 you can do almost anything.

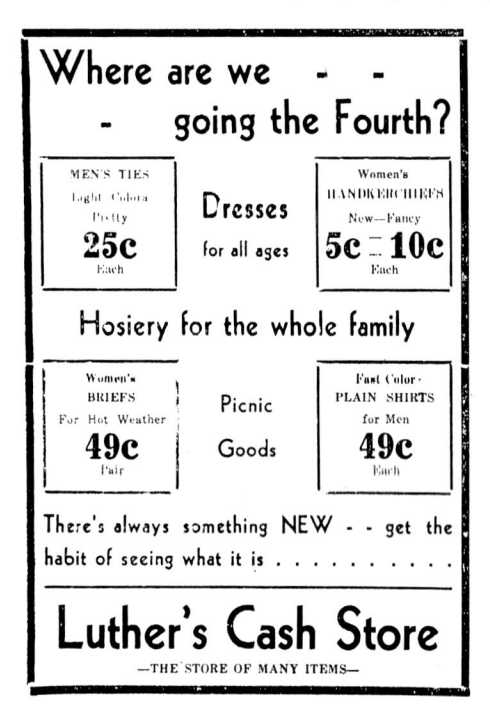

Where are we - - - going the Fourth?

| MEN'S TIES Light Colors Pretty **25c** Each | Dresses for all ages | Women's HANDKERCHIEFS New—Fancy **5c - 10c** Each |

Hosiery for the whole family

| Women's BRIEFS For Hot Weather **49c** Pair | Picnic Goods | Fast Color PLAIN SHIRTS for Men **49c** Each |

There's always something NEW - - get the habit of seeing what it is . . . .

Luther's Cash Store
—THE STORE OF MANY ITEMS—

Waterville's Biggest Business

We often don't think of schooling as a business but it was and still is the biggest single business in Waterville.

In 1889 the school teachers that returned for the 1889-1890 school year were **Enid Smith, Louise Moulton, Helen Winers, Mary Devany, Lillie M. Turrittin** and **Ida Sheldon.**

In 1965 the high school teachers returning were **George Barnard, Thomas Bengston, Don Bohn, Ernest Dahl, Meredith Kelley, Mabel Mende, Lawrence Meskan, Don Plumhoff, Del Pope, June Sautbine, Dean Wilkes, Herman Winkels, Lorraine Wolverton.** The new teachers were **Milan Behr, Joe Burns, Arnold Kruzmark, Lorraine Lymburn, Otto Luknic, Carol Miller, John Ruohonieme, Bill Sautbine, Bill Slattery** and **Jerome Wisdorf.**

John Dudley, Don Bohn, Jim Balfe, Mason Marzahn, Herman Hunte formed Waterville Lions Club. (1945)

Waterville Furniture Factory

The **John Babcock** Furniture Factory was built in the middle 1850's. The original wooden structure was destroyed by fire in the 1870's and a brick building was erected in its place. **L.Z. Rogers** purchased the building in 1887 and operated it on a larger scale. It was later under the management of the Peterson Art Company.

No. 5173—Waterville Furniture Co.

Cannon Valley Telephone Exchange.

The Great White Way—Corcoran's

Dave Corcoran was an innovator. In 1899 he added a popcorn and peanut roaster. He made candy, sold ice cream, made the cones and had three stores in one. He was the first to put in street lights in front and it became "The Great White Way."

Do you remember the ceiling fans in Corcoran's? They were put in around 1917 when **Dave** raised the ceiling and remodeled the place. **Ed Courtney** married **Dave's** daughter, **Irene**. **Ed** would eventually manage the store. In this photo, **Irene** is having a birthday party. She invited anyone who wished to attend. **Irene** was a popular girl and her dad's store was a popular store.

Some of **Dave's** employees were his wife, **Caroline Corcoran**, and **Nora Sanford** and **May Straub**. **Molly Preuss** and **Mrs. Moose Watzek** worked later at **Courtney's** as did **Mel Schulz**. As a boy in the 1940's, **Mel** would start the fires in **Courtney's** and make oat meal and toast for **Gene Spears**.

Joe Lauer won the Christmas lighting contest. The Ralph Sheehy home and the Marvin Wetzel home tied for second. (1961)

Greetings From Waterville, Minn.

Fishing for ice

It was a cold, wet, and heavy work laden business. **Louis Spooner** and his father, **Henry**, are in this picture of a Lake Sakatah ice harvest. For many years, **Henry**, drove **Dr. Theodore Holtan** on his calls to patients in this area. **Henry** died in June of 1957. **Louis** had retired to Florida. They both worked for **Carl** and son, **Paul Stavenau**. In the days of the ice boxes, ice was a prime commodity.

Other men that worked for **Stavanau** were **Jake Younger, George Kritzer, Adolph Werth, Emil Huebl, Emil Schwartz, Ole Iverson,** and **Carl Mertins**.

The ice was harvested on the south shore of Lake Sakatah. Cakes of ice equalling about 125-150 pounds were loaded on conveyor belts and then into boxcars. Once the ice was harvested it was stored in **Carl Stavenau's** ice house located at the north end of Mill Street.

Waterville's pure water

Imagine those dog days of August in the 1930's when the temperature hits 90 for several days, the humidity causes walls to sweat, and even the algae laden lakes look hot. **Lyle Miller, George Moench, Minie Van Fleet** and **Frank Comstock** and everyone else are talking about the heat. More than one are saying how nice it would be to take time out to visit **Stavenau's** ice house, wipe the sawdust off a large chunk, chip off a piece and press it to your face. It was at that time Watervillians really appreciated the ice harvesters.

Waterville ice was loaded in box cars as shown in this photo and shipped to various cities to supply them with ice for their ice boxes and ice for their lemonade. Naturally, Waterville kept its own supply of ice that was insulated with sawdust and stored in the ice house.

Delivering ice to the homes in the summer for **Carl** and **Paul Stavenau** was a daily ritual. A cake of ice might last a day or more only to be replaced by another. Pure Waterville water supplied the ice for those cool summer drinks that were the envy of the plains people.

Twins were born to Mr. and Mrs. Stan Blowers. (1952)

Waterville Meats

*E*very town had a butcher shop and Waterville had one of the best in **John Dawald's** meats. Later **Lester Comstock** would maintain the tradition in his shop on the opposite side of the street. **John's** shop was located in the same building that would later occupy the O.K. Cafe.

John will get some business from visitors who have to come to town to attend the funeral of **George Cram**. **George** came to Waterville in 1868 with his parents to become one of the most successful farmers in the area—another big business for Waterville. **George** was born in 1856 and died in 1914. **George** and his wife, **Jennie**, had five sons, **Fred, George, William, Hiram** and **Cleveland** and two daughters, **Mrs. William Gish** and **Miss Gladys.** The funeral attendance at the U.B. Church was one of the largest ever seen. **George** was a man of unquestionable integrity.

E. M. Lawless resigned the cashiership of the Security State Bank to take active charge of the Waterville *Sentinel* newspaper. **W.L. Warburton** replaced him.

Lakeside Sanitary Dairy

*T*his early 1900 dairy was operated by **P. O'Leary** and sons. **P. O'Leary** was also one of Waterville's local historians. He wrote an early piece for the *Advance* describing the *Early History of Waterville*.

Most communities of Waterville's size had their local dairy. Waterville's Tetonka Dairy operated for many years. **Harry Greer** would deliver the milk and butter to the various stores in town in the 1950's. There was also home delivery.

Perhaps some of you still possess one of the Tetonka Dairy quart glass bottles. "Pasteurized milk and cream, Tetonka Dairy" was embossed on the bottle. On the other side of the bottle it read, "Baby knows best! Milk is good for grown-ups too." The cardboard milk cap had a picture of an Indian chief. Remember?

This photo is taken in front of **Dave Corcoran's** restaurant. **Dave** will pay cash for your butter and eggs. While you are there, pick up some of his Jack Spratt Jello on sale for ten cents per package.

Nellie Spooner, Vera Wetzel, Donald Marsh, Paul Schwichtenberg, Jean Monson, Hubert Moench, Don Miller graduate from WHS. (1932)

A real fish story—100 Tons

It's a 10 degree day, the skies are clear and some of Waterville's best commercial fishermen are emptying their nets. It has been a good haul—one of the best of the season.

That's **Frank Dusbabek** standing in the back row. He's the fifth person from the right. When he heard the news he had to come and take a look. There is something about a lot of fish that attracts a crowd.

Waterville always had commercial fishermen. The names of **Sikel, Bittrich, Mertins** and **Geyers** come to mind. There were many others.

This photo, taken in 1937, appears to be on Lake Tetonka.

Everybody seems to be holding a fish and having a good time. The boxes in the back will all be full by night fall and some pretty happy fishermen will be counting fish in their sleep.

Grandpa Higgins

"The death of **J.S. Higgins**," reported in the June 26, 1914 *Sentinel*, "in this city this week removes from our midst a link that connected us with the nations's early youth. . . . those pioneer times that tested the fiber and metal of men."

Early residents here remember the wilderness that surrounded Waterville when **Mr. Higgins** came here in the 1870's. Even some of us who belong to a younger generation can recall the heavy forests and the untamed condition of this country not so many years ago.

Joshua S. Higgins died at his home in West Waterville on June 24, 1914. He was born in Connecticut on September 23, 1819. He came to Waterville in 1875. He built a sawmill in West Waterville and it became a successful business for many years. He left two surviving grandsons, **Byron J.** and **Leslie M. Fowler** both of Waterville.

Mr. Higgins had voted in every presidential election for seventy-two years, having cast his first vote for William Henry Harrison in 1840.

Mrs. Hazel Amundson says that more books are being checked out of the public library due to the interest in answering the $64,000 questions. (1957)

Greetings From Waterville, Minn.

Big apples at Mammoth Store

On sale at the Mammoth Dept. Store in 1911 were brassieres for 25 cents. Also for sale at the Mammoth Store were apples. This photo was taken in the early 1900's.

The first building of **L.Z. Rogers** was destroyed by fire in 1861. He at once rebuilt and enlarged his business until the store covered a half block and this he conducted until he sold the business to his son-in-law **George**.

George Greene served as a clerk for **L.Z. Rogers**, the owner of **Rogers'** Store, for 24 years. In 1885 he married **Rogers'** daughter, **Ellen**. Being a member of the family helped, no doubt, when later, he and a **Mr. Bliss**, bought the business. I imagine at this time in the early 1900's it became known as the Mammoth Department Store. **Mr. Bliss** purchased the grocery and hardware departments and **Mr. Greene** bought the other departments.

In 1904 **George Greene**, his father, **William Greene**, and attorney **Mahlon Evertt** organized the first bank in Waterville— the First National Bank of Waterville.

Clothing/Bowling/Antiques

The **George E. Greene** store advertised on the back of its receipt pads, "Henderson corsets in all styles to fit the form. If anything is wrong tell us; if all right tell your neighbors." In 1911, a **Mrs. Mark Sheehy** purchased 3 pair of socks for 25 cents, 3 vests for $1.50, and 2 pairs of pajamas for $1.00.

The photo shows the mother of **Betty Schwartz**. She is chatting with a clerk about the quality of the apples on sale. She wondered where **Mr. Greene** had purchased them.

E.J. Ebling bought the store around 1920. In 1933, **Ebling** had Buster Playsuits for children for 49 cents and mosquito netting for 12 cents per yard. I'm not sure when **Ebling** sold the building but it later became a bowling alley operated by **Ken Buck** and then later by **Jack Salzle**.

In June of 1957 **John Nelson** and **Gilbert Wirig** were partners in the furniture business in this building. They remodeled the building formerly occupied by the bowling alley..

Curt Wetzel and **Lori Stangler** now own "The Attic" antique shop located in one of Waterville's oldest buildings.

Mr. and Mrs. Henry Bosacker celebrated their 50th wedding anniversary at Trinity Lutheran Church. (1956)

Greetings From Waterville, Minn.

Golfing on the shores of Lake Tetonka

That's **Bill** and **June Sautbine** on their golf course located on the west side of Antl's Bay on Lake Tetonka.. The golf course added a new dimension to the recreation life of Watervillians in the early '60's. Both **Bill** and **June** are educators and taught at Waterville High School. **June** was a physical education teacher in Waterville for many years.

June is talking to **Bill** about the School Health and Safety Workshop she will be attending at Camp Lake Herbert near Brainerd. **Bill** is trying to concentrate on the putt. Yes, he did make it.

Fish for sale and Centennial

Walt Mertins was one of many people in Waterville over the years who made fish their livelihood. His business on the north side of Lake Sakatah was a prime location for those Iowa fishermen who came to fish bullheads but didn't catch any.

The first fish market was located where **Katie Ranshaw** lived on the southwest corner of Lake Sakatah. It was managed by **Jim Buell**, a Civil War veteran. When he died, **"Poley" Beach** took it over.

Rudy Ebert won the best goatee contest for the Waterville Centennial at about the time this photo was taken in 1957. **Howard Coon** was in the running for the full beard contest. **Louis Grassinger** won second place in the fanciest facial adornment contest. **Bert Beach** was the second oldest native son. He was still active as City Recorder and Weighmaster at City Hall. **Elsie Francisco** at 77 was the oldest person present.

Other news in town in 1957 tells us that **Elaine Meinke** is a new employee at the Security State Bank. **Craig Conners** is recovering from surgery at St. Lucas Hospital.

Denny Grover has been tracking the cougar that has been seen in the area. (1959)

Page 6-10

Greetings From Waterville, Minn.

Paul Zollner's Feed & Backman's

Zollner's Feed Mill was located south of **Fahning's** on the other side of the Chicago Great Western Railroad tracks. **Paul Zollner** operated the mill with his father from 1924-1941. In 1941, **Paul** took over the operation of the mill.

No doubt **Mr. Zollner** did business with **Charles Backman** who owned **Backman** Produce on Main Street — another prominent Waterville business (see *Section 1*). According to **Mort Mengis, Charles Backman** bought out the business of a **Mr. A.J. Wagner** who had a poultry and egg business in the old Waterville *Gazette* building, located about where the Backman Produce building is located. A chair factory was also located in this same area.

The men that served as pallbearers for **Mrs. Jim Lawless** in 1957 who died at 87 will remember **Zollner's** mill: **Bill Luther, Cleve Cram, Jim Balfe, Charles Grubish** and **Wm. Nadeau**.

Bob Cribbs is county chairman of the LeSueur county blood program.

Page 6-11

Greetings From Waterville, Minn.

PICKLE FACTORY

Waterville Pickle Factory

I now know why my mother was able to make such good dill pickles—it's part of Waterville's heritage.

The Gedney Pickle Factory was located in the vicinity of where Northrup King had their factory. Looking north in this photograph, you can see the smoke stacks near the water works and the furniture factory.

Citizens of Waterville were often reminded to bring their pickles to the factory in the summer for processing.

When this photograph was taken in the 1920's, people were talking about the five dollar bill that **Mrs. Carl Kisor** found in **Corcoran's** restaurant and advertised in the *Advance*. **Clifford Powell** read the advertisement and called **Mr. Kisor**. People were speculating as to the amount of the reward.

I think I now know why Waterville people have always been so honest—dill pickles.

17¢

Cash or Trade paid for your Eggs

The more you bring in the more you can buy. Remember

CASH OR TRADE

17¢

R.R. RILEY

"The People's Store"

Lt. John Raedeke receives Air Medal for coolness, courage and skill while participating in bomber combat missions in Europe. (1944)

Greetings From Waterville, Minn.

If you tell them, they will come.

Bullhead Fishing Capital of the World
Waterville, Minnesota

A reason to be proud

There would be no resorts in Waterville had it not been for the bullhead. When Waterville citizens decided to market this frightful, but friendly yellow bellied fellow, they also sold people on Waterville. When people came to Waterville to fish the bullhead, they needed a place to stay. At the best of times, there were more than two dozen resorts in Waterville—all catering to the Waterville bullhead. And, why not? You could catch them faster than you could bait your hook and you could eat them as fast as they were taken out of the frying pan. That's a good combination.

Roger Preuss has a lot to do with making the bullhead Waterville's official mascot. He has earned worldwide respect for his wildlife paintings—of which there are many. But, to the citizens of Waterville, its native son's most respected painting will be the official portrait of the Waterville bullhead.

Roger Preuss deisgned the federal duck stamp. (1949)

Page 7-1

Greetings From Waterville, Minn.

What a better place to stay

What was the only resort located on the south side of upper Sakatah? It was called "The Oaks Resort." **C.H. Bliss** was the proprietor of this Lake Sakatah resort located among the oaks on the hill. Some of the buildings still remain. **Herman Solyntjes** stayed in one of the cottages during the summer of 1929 when his father **Pete** and his family came to Waterville. Cottages often served a dual purpose. If they could not be rented out to tourists, resort owners rented them to residents looking for temporary housing. And, what a better place to stay than near a lake.

They're in, Knot

Mr. Bliss gave his cottages interesting names: Seldom Inn, Knot Inn, and Never Inn. No doubt **Mr. Bliss** hoped that the fish would be biting so the clients would be on the lake filling their five gallon pails with bullheads and not in their cabins wishing they had gone somewhere else.

Notice the small child pictured in the shade under the oaks. If the child is still living,, do you suppose she has any recollection of her summer in Waterville in the 1920's? The child was probably a relative of **Mr. Bliss**—perhaps a daughter?

Photographer **Ryan** would often take his postcard photos with the owner or members of the owner's family in the cards.

Ryan used a good marketing strategy in this 1920's photo.

Rosanne Schmidt, Miss Waterville of 1957, appeared in the Nicollet Parade. (1957)

Page 7-2

Resort owners like Mr. Bliss rest with sleeves rolled-up

There doesn't appear to be too much activity today on Lake Sakatah. Maybe the fishermen have come in for lunch or it's those dog days of August when the fish are about as inactive as the people.

Saltzmans would later claim ownership to "The Oaks."

Well, there's **Mr. Bliss** taking a minute to sit on the steps leading down to the boats. I wonder what's on his mind? "Maybe I should invest in a couple of outboards to rent with the boats." Or, "I need to patch a few boats before someone complains."

When **Bert Ryan** made the appointment to come and take photos of his resort, **Mr. Bliss** probably figured this investment would be his marketing strategy for the year. He chose to wear a bow tie to give viewers the business look while at the same time having his sleeves rolled up would also give potential guests the idea that he would work hard to make them comfortable. I hope he succeeded.

LeRoy Raedeke has a 10 x 12 new building for sale that would make a nice lake cottage. Call 13F21. (1956)

Greetings From Waterville, Minn.

Getting ready for company

It was still called "The Oaks" in the 1950's. Visitors were expected to fill the cabins at Waterville's resorts this week-end in celebration of the Waterville Centennial. One of the big attractions would be the Miss Waterville Queen title. The ten contestants were **Joan Radcliff, Pat Schwichtenberg, Judy Balfe, Rosanne Schmidt, Pat Murker, Colleen Greer, Pat Hebl, Kathy Salmon, Carol Schwichtenberg,** and **Margaret Lamont.**

Retail stores in Waterville would close at noon on Saturday, June 14, 1957. **Tom Abbott** was in charge of the parade. The parade would form in front of the school. He expected about 75 units.

The Oaks was conveniently located for parade goers.

You can still "Come in"

It's no longer "The Oaks" and "Seldom Inn" and "Knot Inn" are not in but you can still come in and rent cabins from **Florence Saltzman** who manages the resort. She and her husband, **Henry**, came north from Des Moines in 1966 and purchased the resort from **Sid Troughtner**. **Sid** purchased it from a **Mr. Dietz** in the 50's.

Florence still gets guests from many parts of the United States to stay at **Saltzman's** South Side Resort where a cool north breeze and shade from giant oaks still greet tourists as they did 70 years ago. When you add congeniality and good fishing, you can entice most people to come almost anywhere.

Elmer Dusbabek will be working the hand pumper of an old piece of fire equipment in the Centennial parade. (1957)

Greetings From Waterville, Minn.

It will always be Hoban's to me

To this day, I still refer to Best Point Resort as **Hoban's**. Best Point first started as **Hoban's** Best Point in the early 1920's. It changed its name to "Best Point" in 1951.

In this 1920's photo, spring arrived not too long ago. The ice is out and the docks will soon be in the lake. It has only been a few years since the resort has opened. It will become a very fine resort that will hold many memories for many people.

Rest for the weary and worried

Best Point Resort, to me, was the resort's resort. It was secluded on the southwest shore of Lake Tetonka, down a steep hill with a snake-like drive that led to a beautiful point. It was kind of a natural hideaway for tourists and a very peaceful setting for people who wanted to leave their worries behind.

Maybe some of the guests that attended the **Henry Pommeranz** funeral this past week (1956) stayed at **Hoban's**. They were probably a bit weary from traveling. **Henry** came to the U.S. by boat in 1892 from Germany. **Henry**, just a baby, became very ill on the way over. His mother, **Marie**, thought he was dead but concealed him because she didn't want to see him buried at sea. At the end of the voyage it was discovered he was still alive. **Henry** farmed south of town, later worked at **Fahnings** and was a very active member of Lakeside Methodist. He married **Adeline Marzahn**. **Frank Knish, Henry Stoering, Jack Johnson, Ed Zitzman, Ben Borchardt,** and **Emil Schwartz** were pallbearers at the funeral.

Della Schmidtke bowled a 181. (1956)

Greetings From Waterville, Minn.

The Hamms' Beer sign still remains

Right off of the point is one of the deepest places in Lake Tetonka—about 40 feet. It also seemed like the coldest when you had to stand out on the ice and wait for the crappies to bite. Many times my father would take my brother and me ice fishing out to **Hoban's**. It was great when the fish did bite but not so great when you had to pull in 40 feet of line with a cold wind blowing.

In the summer of '94, my father and I drove out to Best Point. It is one of only two resorts remaining on Lake Tetonka today. **Jerry and Linda Miller** are the current owners.

Some things never change. It still is one of the most scenic places on the Lake and the Hamms' Beer Sign still hangs from the same tree as it was in this 1950's photo.

Put in a couple of gallons

I suppose it was quite a thing to drive your boat next to a dock with a gasoline pump on it. Because the distance from Best Point to the nearest gasoline pumps in Waterville was more than just a few miles, putting a pump on the dock was probably a necessity. To the left of the pump on the other side of the lake, you can see the home of **Don Werner**.

Well it's a warm, sunny day on Lake Tetonka. There are some children swimming in the calm waters—probably trying to catch some minnows.

The Iowa tourists were happy to learn this week of the pond for rearing fish that was completed on the **Norman Findahl** farm this week. The local sportsman club helped. Current 1952 officers are **Paul Schulz, Art Roeglin, Jim Balfe, Glenn Preuss, Bob Culhane, Sr., Steve Halek, and Fritz Taylor.**

There is a certain magic about water that entices people to get close to it. It sort of has a freeing of the spirit effect. Iowans will be in good spirits when the fish in the fish pond are freed.

Art Ranshaw was re-elected mayor. (1952)

Page 7-6

Greetings From Waterville, Minn.

Creating a good impression

This card of **Otto Pope's** resort was sent to **Opal Walker** of St. Charles, Minnesota. It read, "I was up here in August of 1923. Our cottage was the third one."

Vacationers must have taken some pride in the cottage they stayed in to point it out to friends. **Otto**, standing in front of the second cottage, no doubt, took great pride in keeping his cottages in good clean condition. Marketing in the early days of the resort business was mostly by word of mouth. It was important to resort owners to have visitors leave with a good impression. No doubt, **Otto** worked hard at this.

It looks like spring is here and he is getting ready for visitors from the south and other places who don't have the privilege of living near water.

In 1953 **Otto Pope** ran an ad in the *Advance* where he advertised a closing out sale of his summer resort. He had 10 14X20 cottages for sale and 7 Frigidaires.

Otto Pope Injured Fatally In Accident

Otto Pope purchased this resort in 1921 and managed it until **McWhirter** purchased it and named it "Lakeview Resort." Headlines in the August 7, 1957 *Advance* read, "**Mr. and Mrs. Otto Pope** Injured Fatally In Accident." **Otto** was driving a 1949 Nash that was struck by a 1951 Buick at the intersection of Highways 13 and 60 at one o'clock in the afternoon. They were on their way to visit their son-in-law, **Roman Grubish**. **Otto** was 84 and **Esther** was 77.

The bridge that eventually would separate Lower Sakatah from Upper Sakatah has not been built. On the west side of the lake is the Waterville Furniture Factory. There are two large, three story brick buildings that had their own water tower.

If you look closely, you can see **Otto** with the hand sickle on the left side of the road in the weeds. **Esther** has been after him to get rid of those unsightly weeds by the path to the boats.

Mr. and Mrs. Perry Pope and family were Sunday afternoon visitors at the home of Mr. and Mrs. Fred Stavenau. (1944)

Greetings From Waterville, Minn.

Marvelous McWhirter's Lakeview Resort

Located on the north side of Lake Sakatah, **McWhirter** Lakeview Resort provided boats, cabins and even lunch.

Newton, Iowa farmers, **Robert** and **Zelpha McWhirter** purchased the resort formerly owned by **Otto Pope**. They bought it from **Mr.** and **Mrs. Ralph Waterman** in 1957. Three cabins were moved to the resort from Sakatah State Park during the winter when the ice was frozen. When **Zelpha** served lunch, she called the sandwiches Z-burgers. She celebrated her 94th birthday on June 28, 1993.

"I love it here. It's my whole life." **Zelpha's** comment is a testimony to the fact that Iowa farmers have served Waterville well.

What a great location!

When the bridge was constructed dividing Lake Sakatah, **McWhirter's** Resort was the first resort travelers saw as they entered Waterville from the north. The large shaded area that provided a nice view of the lake as well as the city was an attractive feature.

Zelpha said she never had any trouble with any of her resort people and they never stole anything. **Bob** died in 1980 but **Zelpha** kept up the **McWhirter** tradition by keeping the resort open for its regular customers and other travelers who chose to stay in the blue cottages under blue skies in the land of the sky blue waters.

Don Barrett sold his Motor Company to Theron Johnston. (1950)

The parents of Adolph Dehn also left their mark

The parents of nationally known Waterville artist, **Adolph Dehn**, built the cabins at **Vincent Wilmes** Resort. It was also known as **Ward's** Resort. They owned it after **Dehn** and before **Wilmes**. One or two of the cottages still remain.

The people in this 1920's photo appear to be enjoying themselves. But, then again, it's hard not to enjoy yourself when you are on the shores of Lake Tetonka.

Some of the women have been contemplating going to town to look over the *Henderson Rub-R-Ride* reducing girdle they heard was on sale at **Eblings** store. That is, if the fish aren't biting.

Night crawlers: one cent each

When **Ward's** owned the resort, my brother, **Craig**, **Joe Bittrich** and I would sell **Mr. Ward** night crawlers at a penny apiece. Not only did they sell night crawlers, there was also a cafe. "Come to **Lucille** and **Marlowe's** Lakeview Cafe at **Ward's** resort" was an ad in a 1940's *Advance*. They offered fish frys and club steaks every day.

It's 1940 and people were sad to learn of the death of **Mrs. Pete Solyntjes** but happy to learn of the recent marriage of **Mr. John Frodl** who was married in Minneapolis.

Oh, yes, those are the night crawler hunters to the right. **John** and **Craig Eggers** on the left and **Roland Bittrich** on the right. It was the first day of kindergarten for **Craig** and **Roland**. Were they thinking about nightcrawlers or the ABC's?

Bud Wilcox passed away. (1960)

Greetings From Waterville, Minn.

A shady place to take a rest

Located on the north end of Herbert Street and on the southeast shore of Lake Tetonka, **Wilmes** Resort offered a shady rest spot for vacationers. If they didn't find any action on the lake, they could always find something happening at near-by **Osborn's** Dam.

Visitors have been telling each other of the last 1957 summer band concert to be offered this evening down town. **Mr. Tom Abbott** and the Waterville High School band have been conducting a number of concerts this summer. **Mr. Abbott** wishes to thank **Dr. Rieke, Jim Balfe, Hap Watzek** and **Richard Wong's** O.K. Cafe for providing the treats after the concerts.

It was a quieter time

Sitting on the lawn of **Wilmes'** Resort in the '50's are **Jennifer** and **Gretchen Rausch** and a friend. The fifties were a quieter time. There was time to catch your breath, to sit on the lawn in the sunshine. They wanted to go swimming today at the beach but **Mr. Tietz**, swimming instructor, has closed the beach for the day. The water is beginning to get on the "green" side.

At the very end of the road is a mailbox—how convenient.

Art Sorgatz has a Mossberg automatic rifle for sale. (1952)

Greetings From Waterville, Minn.

If only trees could talk

McPeek's point was two miles west of Waterville off of Highway 13. Located on the north side of the lake, it was also known as Tetonka Park On July 4, 1896, the **Andrew's** Opera Company opened in their location a little to the west.

Imagine a lazy July Sunday afternoon in the 1890's. Having taken the train from town, men and women dressed in hats and white shirts and dresses are picnicking among the shade trees. They are waiting to view the opera that will soon be performing on a platform located in the small bay (where the boats are). Some are getting a bite to eat before the horse races begin, others are taking a steamboat excursion, some are watching the yachting races and others listen to one of two bands. There will be fireworks in the evening.

Waterville in the 1890's was gaining quite a reputation as a summer tourist mecca. And, why not? A train would take you from a hot, dusty depot to shade and serenity in a matter of minutes. Wouldn't you like to spend one day in Waterville in the 1890's?

A very nice gentleman

Mary Lou Solyntjes would walk to **McPeek's** Point from school on occasion. She would walk one mile up the north side to the railroad bridge and then west one mile to Tetonka Homes Resort and **McPeek's** Point. (Be careful of the trains **Mary Lou**.)

Mary Lou's dad, **Frank Luker** said that **Mr. McPeek** was a very nice gentleman with a great sense of humor. When **McPeek** died in 1923, his wife **Laura** married a **Mr. Giles** that used to play in the band along with **Hiller Teff**. The **Giles'** lived over the Gamble Store.

Mr. McPeek is pictured petting the dog. You can see **Lucinda Beach's** clothes on the line to the right and in the background. **Lucinda** is **Mary Lou's** mother. It must be Monday.

Mr. and Mrs. Peter Rakume were run down by a passenger train and killed. (1915)

Page 7-11

Greetings From Waterville, Minn.

When women wore white dresses

The house you see in the background is still standing. **Al Werner** lived in it until recent years. The **Frank Luker** buildings are also in the background. The old race track horse barn that existed during the time of the **Andrew's** Opera House is between the trees.

I don't know who the women are in the white dresses. They could be members of the **McPeek** family or they could be guests. People generally dressed up to have their picture taken. So, this definitely was a special occasion. Little did they know they would be included in a history of Waterville book. So, I guess it was a special occasion.

The second building from the left is where the Opera Company sold drinks. If you follow the road you will see the 90 foot horse barn in the back that was home to the race horses.

The sunfish are biting

This card was mailed from Morristown in 1919. The note on the back of the card read, "We are enjoying camp life and getting all kinds of fish. We were all out in a boat on the lake last evening for a couple of hours and we caught some fifty sunfish and perch. Lydia caught 19 of them."

Some things never change. People like to catch fish and after they catch them they tell others.

They still need boats for the boat parade to be held at 9:00 p.m. on Saturday, July 4, 1959 as part of Waterville's Waterama. If you do wish to join the parade, contact **Earl Fritz, Don Werner, Charles Slechta, Ken Slechta, Merle Grubbish** or **Willard Goltz**.

Nancy Bohn is attending Girls State. Damaris Fredell is a student at St. Barnabas School of Nursing. (1959)

Greetings From Waterville, Minn.

That's Frank Luker second from the left

Frank built six cabins from some of the lumber that was part of the horse barn from the old racetrack. **Luker's** purchased the buildings in 1919 from **McPeek**. They made it into a resort and also sold gravel.

"Well I am having a good time. I arrived here at 4:30 and got 13 big bullheads the first night and 5 silver bass. Sure am having fun. Caught the fish from shore." That was the note sent from Waterville in 1944 to someone in Mason City, Iowa.

Let's go to Comeaux's, Land of the Sky Blue Waters

Al and **Vi Comeaux** purchased Tetonka Homes from a **Mrs. Pratt** in 1951 and owned it for about 20 years. The place was always known as **Comeaux's** to me. It was quite a gathering place on Sunday afternoons. **Al** had a shuffle board, bowling machine in the resort office and they were also permitted to serve 3-2 beer on Sunday. I can still see the lighted Hamm's beer sign on the wall with its shimmering sky blue waters.

Al and **Vi** had seven cabins on this piece of land that was some of the best on Lake Tetonka. **Al Werner** lived to the west and owned the Our Own Hardware store in town. He also had another piece of nice property. At one time, **Al** said he could have purchased **Werner's** seven acres for $4500.

Yes, going out to **Comeaux's** on a Sunday afternoon to play shuffleboard bowling, listening to fish stories and watching the Hamm's Beer sign with its shimmering waters—life couldn't get much better.

Mr. and Mrs. Marvin Wetzel had a baby boy on April 1. (1952)

Greetings From Waterville, Minn.

Dance at Doc's Place

Maplewood Park was located on the east side of Lake Tetonka. In this early 1900's photo, there was a K.C. picnic held at Maplewood Park. The boys on the shore are wearing knickers, the women are in their white dresses and the men in the water are having some kind of race or game with wash tubs.

There are not too many references to Maplewood Park. One ad in the *Advance* stated, "Come and dance at **Doc's** Place, formerly Maplewood Park."

It has been a few years since the Andrews Opera Company left town. People still talk about the good times at the race track and the kids miss the fireworks. "One thing about Maplewood Park," people say,"It's a lot cheaper."

Now playing: Ray Stolzenberg and his Northern Playboys

Brady's Silver Streak Pavilion featuring Ray Stolzenberg and his Northern Playboys was advertised in the June 9, 1945 *Advance*. The Pavilion referred to in this ad was located on the east side of Lake Tetonka. at **Stavenau's** and later, **Doc's** Place.

The pavilion featured Whoppee John, Six Fat Dutchmen and other big bands that drew big crowds. Every Thursday night was dancing. Roller skating was several nights per week.

There's a lot of war news around Waterville in the 40's. Much of the talk at the Pavilion is about people in the war or going to war. **Lt. Roger Findahl** is home on furlough. **Ralph Hagel** is at the U.S. Naval Training Center in Illinois. **Ray Kalow** is in the South Pacific.

The dancers dance to Whoopee John and Whoopee John's rendition of a Glenn Miller tune and the talk is up-beat but their thoughts are of their brothers and sisters in the war.

S/Sgt. Eugene Prehn was a Flying Fortress gunner in Europe for six months for 30 missions. (1944)

Greetings From Waterville, Minn.

The place hasn't changed much

The **Brady's** purchased the site from **Ed Stavenau** in 1944. This included 8 acres, house, dance pavilion and 8 cabins. They added a 9th cabin later.

When you drive on the east side of Lake Tetonka today, the place hasn't changed that much. The homes have been remodeled and the Silver Streak is gone but you can still envision what it was like sixty years ago.

The brown house next to the cabins belonged to **Farrington's**. **Louis Dusbabek,** builder of the original resort, sold it to **Mr. Utley** (father of **Bea Sherratt**) then to **Ed Stavenau** then to **Brady's**.

This postcard was sent to **Sgt. David Atherton** of Waterville in 1943 who was stationed at Camp Shelby in Mississippi. "I imagine you have the girls' heart in a whirlwind; take it easy."

Good news and bad news

That's **Mr. Brady** standing on the left. Behind him is the Silver Streak Pavilion and to the right is the home that is now occupied by **Bruce** and **Ruth Commins**.

It's in the 1920's and several deaths are the talk around town. **Harry Stowe** was elected alderman to fill the vacancy caused by the death of Alderman **Fred Fuller**.

Mrs. William Christjaner went to Nebraska due to the death of her father, **Mr. John Backman**. And, **Mr. Richard Peach** died on September 21, 1924.

On the bright side, people are happy for Robert Todd Lincoln who celebrated his 82nd birthday—the son and only surviving descendant of Abraham Lincoln.

A.L. Ewer is now doing the delivering for all the grocery men in town. (1904)

Greetings From Waterville, Minn.

One month for 45 dollars

How much did a stay at a resort cost in the thirties? This card was addressed to a **Mrs. Good** in Cedar Rapids and sent from **Doc's** place in 1932. A cottage was for four people with box spring and everything furnished except ice, oil and towels. A boat came with the cottage. One week was $14.00, two weeks were $26.00, and one month was $45.00.

We don't know if **Mrs. Good** and her family did stay at **Doc's** place. But it was quite a bargain: sandy beach, boats, modern furnished cabins and dancing and roller skating at the Silver Streak. Phone 215, make your reservations today and don't delay.

Aluminum boats and lawn chairs

The wooden boats have been replaced by aluminum boats. The wooden benches have been replaced by steel lawn chairs. **Brady's** sold the resort to a **Mr. Hurst** and it is now called Hillside Resort. **Hurst** will eventually sell the cabins to **John L. Hrdlicka, Pete Solyntjes** and **Frank Luker** in 1950.

Steel lawn chairs don't have to be recovered but lamp shades do. This is what the Merry Homemakers were up to in Waterville in January of 1955 at the farm home of **Mrs. Earl Fritz**. **Mrs. Gordon Miller** and **Mrs. Melvin Meyer** presented the topic. The next lesson will be on "keeping fit" and it will be presented at the home of **Mrs. Lyle Miller**. **Mrs. Gene Stoering** and **Mrs. John Sheehy** had a great lunch that helped everyone forget about lamp shades.

Anna Kelm's was the location for the North Side Club meeting. The club voted to give $3.00 to the Sister Kenny Fund. (1944)

Greetings From Waterville, Minn.

The best thing about vacations

One thing that hasn't changed is the fact that it's hard to keep kids out of the water when on vacation. When they were in water, they had to be watched. The only recourse parents had was to tell kids not to go swimming after they had eaten. Because kids ate all of the time, this wasn't a bad idea.. The other recourse was to take along grandma and grandpa and let them watch the kids. It looks like that is the case in this late 40's photo.

Some kids probably went swimming at the surprise party given for **Melvin Kritzer** in 1945 at his cottage in honor of his 40th birthday. **Melvin** was lying on the couch when guests entered the back door. Surprising **Melvin** were **Mr. and Mrs. Robert Byrne, Mr. and Mrs. Alfred Morris, Mr. and Mrs. George Kritzer, Violett Olson** and **Helen Seljeskog**. Happy birthday, **Melvin**.

It always said "1 Vacancy"

Baldwin's Cottage sign was a welcome sight for me as I walked from town and school during the fifties. The sign always said "1 Vacancy." Perhaps this was their way of saying you better stop now because it may be gone when you return. The resort was located on the corner of Tetonka Boulevard and Cottrill (when Cottrill extended to the lake). Some of the cabins still remain.

Mr. and Mrs. John Sullivan would like to thank those who helped them after the Commercial Hotel fire. (1947)

Greetings From Waterville, Minn.

Pontoon boats are in and new homes too

You could be looking at one of the first pontoon boats on Lake Tetonka.

There were not many photos taken of resorts from the lake. **Baldwin's** resort is in the middle of the photo. On the right is a new home being built and on the far left is the home of **Mr. Patricka**. I always thought **Mr.** and **Mrs. Patricka** had the ideal home—kind of a big cottage on a hill surrounded by a white fence. He worked for the Red Owl Company for many years. When I took over **David Rosenau's** paper route for a summer I would deliver papers to his home but I never recall seeing him. It was always one of my favorite places to stop—a hideaway on a hill.

Pauline, Edmund, Lindsay, Mary

I wonder if these small children remember the summer when they sat on the doorstep of Shadow Lawn cottage number 5 at **Doland's** Resort in the early 1900's to have their picture taken? This card was sent to Dysar, Iowa. Printed on the back are the names of the children: **Pauline Fedder Dollansen, Edmund Hix, Jr., Lindsay Hix,** and **Mary Feddersen** If you are still around, **Pauline, Edmund, Lindsay** and **Mary**, give me a call. I have a picture for you.

Doland's Resort was located on the south side of Lake Tetonka on the north of Cottrill Street.

Wanted to rent—A modern house. Inquire of Edgar Eggers. (1944)

Page 7-18

Stand still!

When the bullheads are biting, it's hard to get kids to sit still and pose for a picture. The boy in this picture was probably saying to himself, "We didn't come here to take pictures, we came here to fish. Let's get going."

Doland's Resort on Lake Tetonka, later to be called **Ryans** and later still to be called **Baldwins**, had cottages and boats for rent. The owner was **J.W. Doland** and his phone number was 117.

Yes, the boy did get his limit of bullheads that day and they were the fat, yellow bellied ones. I would rather have had the picture of him and the bullheads.

A Pontiac carrying extra long fishing poles

They came from Missouri in 1941. I wonder if they ever returned? There was a lot on peoples' minds in the early 40's. Pearl Harbor would be bombed in several months and from the looks on the faces of this Missouri family, things are not right with the world—or maybe the fish aren't biting or the cabin wasn't what they expected or the husband wasn't planning to bring his mother-in-law along.

Well, they had a great time. The kids caught their first sunfish. Grandma went home with a lot to talk about. Mom and Dad took some romantic walks along the lake and even went dancing a few times at the Silver Streak Pavilion. Six months later, Dad would be in the Army as a medic.

Hazel Amundson, Eloise Schwanke entertainted their Sunday School pupils at the home of Phyllis Comstock. (1944)

Page 7-19

Greetings From Waterville, Minn.

Be careful when you walk on the dock

It looks like it is about to rain any minute. When **Bert Ryan** took this photo in the 40's, he must have taken it from the top of the hill where a **Mr. Patricka** would live—where Cottrill now meets Marion Street. Remember, Cottrill used to extend all the way to Lake Tetonka.

When Tetonka Boulevard ran along the south side of Lake Tetonka, parking your boats was a problem for cottage and resort owners. When the road was eliminated, it provided some valuable and needed lake shore property for home owners. No doubt, **Mr. Ryan** of **Ryan's** cottages wished he had use of the land where the road runs in this photo.

Be careful when you walk on the dock.

A cute cottage by the lake

This cottage still stands. Next time you take a drive on the south side of Lake Tetonka, can you find it?

I hope that **Nora Sanford** and **Ernest Tuman** were able to stay in a cottage like this when they were married in May of 1914. **Rev. Stone** performed the double ring ceremony at the home of **Mr.** and **Mrs. Wes Sanford**.

The Union Hotel was completely remodeled and is under the management of J.W. Collins. (1914)

Greetings From Waterville, Minn.

Fred Pischel sells Rocky Point

"**Fred Pischel** has sold Rocky Point containing 16 acres to **Mr. Ed Norton, F.W. Knaak's** son-in-law. It sold for a nice sum and **Mr. Norton** will improve the property. **Mr. Pischel** bought the property for $1.25 an acre and has owned it for 39 years."

This was reported in the June 26, 1895 *Advance* files.

I'm not sure if the paper was referring to the land where Rocky Point Resort was located or Rocky Point on Tetonka or **Antl's** Bay. In either case, it was a good buy.

The couple pictured in this photo are probably the owners of Rocky Point Resort.

Aren't the fish biting?

Taken in August of 1950, the writer of this card said, "It was plenty cool on the lakes and fishing wasn't 'too hot,' but each caught something." I guess that's the reason why none of the boats are being used. It was a common practice to park the boats out from the shore so they wouldn't get washed up on the beach.

In 1914 **Adolph Werth** who has a farm three miles west of town near the Cannon River was lucky to have some water handy. He almost lost his home due to a chimney fire that was spotted by passers by.

Oscar Finke, J. Giles, Jasper Reeb, George Andrus, Will Atherton and Will Quast enlisted in the state militia. (1914)

Greetings From Waterville, Minn.

Wait until we have the pancakes

It started out as a beautiful sunny day during Easter vacation in the 1950's. **Gene Preuss**, brother **Craig**, and I decided to do some camping on this point pictured in this photo. We probably enjoyed a great evening of hamburgers wrapped in tinfoil thrown into the fire, beans, and stories about trapping during the previous winter that we thought was behind us. We were also talking about the pancakes we would make the next morning for breakfast. We woke to find a half inch of ice on our tent with sleet and snow raining on us. **Molly, Gene's** mother, came out to tell us that we should probably wait until summer to resume our camping. I think we said, "Wait until we have our pancakes."

The boats in the picture belong to the resort that is located to the east. **Bob Culhane, Sr**. owned the cows. There are also some horses standing among the trees. Isn't it a great spot for camping?

September can be cold and windy

This is one of the earlier photos of the Rocky Point Fishing and Summer Resort. Cabins were located on both sides of the main house and residence of the owners seen here as the building to the rear of this photo. The cabins are pretty good size, probably all two bedrooms.

This photo card was sent on September 19 of 1938. The writer, a Mrs. Hardon sent this card to Mary Simek of Tama, Iowa. She said "This is a pretty place and plenty of fish to eat. It has been cold and windy but nice this afternoon."

Yes, those middle September days can be cold and windy in Waterville but if the fish are biting, who cares? I don't think Mrs. Hardon did.

Hebl and Gronseth have just completed a large additon to G. G. Cram's barn. (1914)

Greetings From Waterville, Minn.

Smith's Resort - Waterville - Minn

It's not easy

Running a resort is not easy and certainly is not a get-rich-quick scheme. For this reason resorts often changed ownership. In these two look-alike photos, we see that Rocky Point was owned by **Smith** and then **Wulff's** but the photo is the same. Rather than have new photos taken, the old photo was used and the new owner's name (**Wulff**) replaced the previous owner (**Smith**).

What does seem easy is going to Waterville druggist, **J.E. Seidle**, who advertises a simple mixture of buckthorn bark, glycerine, etc., known as Adler-i-ka, the remedy that became famous by curing appendicitis. In 1914 it was a popular commodity.

The family was always friendly

Barb **Wulff**, daughter of **Mr.** and **Mrs. Wulff**, was an excellent singer. She sang at school concerts and for the church. The family was always friendly. For this reason they probably had many vacationers come year after year.

Notice the ice chest in front of the cabin on the left. The telephone pole indicates that these cabins did have electricity so the chest was probably used for something other than keeping things cold.

Rocky Point Resort was located at the very west end of Tetonka Boulevard on the south side of Lake Tetonka. The Rocky Point itself was actually located on the east side of **Antl's** Bay in Lake Tetonka.

Wulff's Resort - Waterville - Minn

Mr. Donald Brandt of the Red Top Cafe submitted to a hernia operation. (1955)

Page 7-23

Greetings From Waterville, Minn.

Sandy Beach Resort

Art Renshaw is sitting in the chair near the house. Son **Tom** is standing to the right. It must be one of those hot and humid days in Waterville because the men have their shirts off. It wouldn't surprise me if they jumped off the dock after this photo was taken—clothes and all.

Sandy Beach Resort had the distinction of having cabins both on Lake Sakatah and on Lake Tetonka. This photo shows the cabin on the west end of Lake Sakatah. The large home is the home of **Art Renshaw**. If you wanted to speak with **Art**, you merely said "59" when the operator asked you, "Number please."

Wouldn't you like to have this wagon?

This is the second half of Sandy Beach Resort located on the east end of Lake Tetonka sandwiched between the public swimming beach and **O'Leary's** cabins. **Art Renshaw** is pretty proud of his station wagon advertising "Sandy Beach Resort." Son, **Tom** and wife, are standing by the sign that reads, "Sandy Beach Resort, **Art Renshaw** and son.

I wonder how business was for **Art** when this 1950's photo was taken? He has the look of confidence as he leans against his wagon. I hope the summer was good for him. Of course resort owners are programed to say, "Fish are biting. Come on down."

Mildred Fredell was the installing officer at the Eastern Star. Nellie Cribbs was the Associate Matron. Darlene Hoban was the Worthy Matron. (1956)   Page 7-24

Greetings From Waterville, Minn.

John O'Leary's Modern Housekeeping Cabins

John O'Leary also owned cabins on both Lake Tetonka and Lake Sakatah and still does. If you are interested, inquire at the Conoco Station. It also is still there.

These particular cabins were situated on the northwest corner of lower Lake Sakatah. You could always find **John** in the station adjacent to the cabins. If you wanted minnows, tackle, guns, outboard motors, a candy bar or if you had to put some air in your bicycle tire, **John** could take care of it for you. He can also give you some tips on where the fish are and aren't.

Getting the boats ready

Here's **John O'Leary** out in his boat near his cabins on the east shore of Lake Tetonka. If you wanted to rent an outboard Evinrude motor, he could do that for you too.

I don't see any boats on the lake. This 1950's photo was probably taken during late July or August when the fish are hard to find. Come evening, however, **John** might find all of his boats heading out towards the Big Rock Pile in **Antl's** Bay where the crappies have been biting.

Mrs. Robert Rausch, Mrs. Don Werner, Mrs. Roman Grubish and Mrs. Ralph Sheehy were drawn for fall term jurors. (1961)

Greetings From Waterville, Minn.

Del's Spruce Lodge

It started with a couple of cabins in 1955 and forty years later you need a map to find your way around Kamp **Dels**. **Del** inherited the tourist business bug from his grandfather, **Otto**. **Del's** son, **Nyl**, is following in his father's footsteps as manager of Kamp **Dels** found on the north side of Lake Sakatah.

People were looking for a place to stay around 1955 when relatives gathered to celebrate Grandmother **Rickard's** 87th birthday. **Don Ellingsworth, Polly** and **Dixie** were there from Minneapolis as were **Ross Ellingworth** and **Harold, Kent,** and **Bobby Rickard** of Waterville.

Neat and clean

I suppose **Perry** and **Inez Pope** had a lot to do with instilling the values of neatness in their kids. Everything is in its place in this 50's photo of Kamp **Dels** or as it was known then as Spruce Lodge Resort. Nothing has changed today in spite of the hundreds of motor homes and an even greater number of campers each weekend. It is still a neat and clean place.

When **Mary Rieke** went to look for her cat in June of 1956 she found it missing. People were to call **Mary** and get a reward if they knew of its whereabouts.

Mary and David have come to live with Mr. and Mrs. Willard Stangler, Curtis and Keith. (1956)

Greetings From Waterville, Minn.

Voices of the CCC

That's a nice mess of bullheads some of **Del's** campers have. When bullheads are biting you can usually catch them anywhere. They probably caught these right off of the dock.

Del's resort business has become more than a nice place to stay for campers, it has also been an employment opportunity for many of Waterville's young people. No doubt if I had been young when Kamp **Del's** began to grow, I would have wanted to work there. I think I would have enjoyed taking care of the animals.

The land that the camp is located on is the former site of the CCC camp that built the Narrow's Bridge and **Osborn's** Dam. When **Del** purchased more land in 1957 and then again in 1965 to expand the camp, he must have heard those voices of yesteryear whispering, "Bring back the camp. Bring back the camp." Well, **Del** did and Waterville is happy he took their advice.

Summer retreats

If you want to get a hold of **Bill Warburton** at his cottage, you can call him at 244. You can also stop at Backman's where he works as bookkeeper.

The south shore of Lake Tetonka was a nice place to retreat to after a hard day's work in the 30's and 40's. My parents rented a cottage next to Bill's for a couple of summers in the early 1940's.

A big catfish, 24 pounds worth, was caught by a Montezuma couple staying at Lym's Resort on Reed's Lake. Many people drove over to see it. **Bill Warburton** may have been one of them in September of 1939.

Mrs. Clell Westgate is looking for school children to room or board. (1939)

Greetings From Waterville, Minn.

Christman's Rest Camp

The card has the look of a real tourist trap. But it's a "trap" that I wished I knew more about. **Christman's** may have been kind of a private camp. It was located east of **Beach's** Point and on the north side of the lake high on a hill. You can see **Beach's** cottage located on the point.

Sakatah Drive looks kind of rugged, doesn't it? It has the look of a real wilderness—exactly what Sakatah Springs Rest Camp owner, **Mr. Christman** wanted you to think.

Who's the Indian Chief?

I believe that **Charles Christman**, the photographer, was the owner of the camp. Only the owner, himself, would take the time to be this creative with the card. Owning cabins must have been the thing to do for photographers because **Burt Ryan**, Waterville's other photographer, also owned cottages. His were on Lake Tetonka.

I wish I knew who was the man dressed in the Indian chief outfit. What do you suppose the "spring water" was? I wouldn't be surprised if one of **Christman's** campers stole his spring water idea and took it to Wall Drug, South Dakota.

In the 1880's, if you were to stand on these hills and look towards the lake you would have seen a steamboat built by **A. Hall**. It was built in Morristown and may have only made one run from Morristown to Waterville via the Cannon River.

Florence Elizabeth Rogers graduated from WHS as valedictorian. (1886)

Page 7-28

Greetings From Waterville, Minn.

Camp Orvida

*N*ow this is what camping is all about. The father is talking over the day's experience with his young son while mom is busy frying fish in the cabin. Dad says, "Yah, that was a good size fish you caught today, son. Tomorrow it wouldn't surprise me if you caught an even bigger one."

"Are we going to eat it tonight?" Dad.

"You bet and Mom is fixing it extra special just for you."

There is something extra special about camping with the family. Camp Orvida at **Christman's** Rest Camp on Lake Sakatah high on a hill was one of the best places to do it.

Wait an hour before swimming

*T*hat's the father and son standing on the dock at sunset on Lake Sakatah. They just finished eating the fish caught earlier in the day. The young one wanted to go swimming but you know what Mom said. "You have to wait at least an hour."

So, father and son are down on the dock just looking.

The boy would have liked to have seen that steamboat about twenty years ago when a **Captain Hall** and his passengers, **Harvey Sandboom, George Breed, Davey Hershey, Bill Wolaver, Walt Cavanaugh, Mr. Virtue, Ben Chapin,** and **Keyes Swift** traveled from Morristown to Waterville. Many places of beauty were passed on the Cannon River: Adam's Bridge, 2nd rifle, Maiden Rock, Kisor's Straight, Deep Hole, Stony Point, Devil Creek, Richter's Spring, Hell's Half Acre, Dingman Straight, and Harper's Ferry, Pike Hole, and The Narrows.

Deaths in Waterville this week: Mrs. C.W. Glotfelter, Mr. James Burns, Don Prehn, Joanne Lee Walburn. (1955)

Greetings From Waterville, Minn.

Small, but the location was nice

No doubt many tourists wrote this on the back of their postcards when they stayed at **Beach's** Cottages. **Wick Beach** was the owner of these cottages located on the north side of Lake Sakatah at the bend in the road at **Beach's** Point. This photo was taken around 1920.

The two deck steamboat that cruised down the Cannon River from Morristown and into Lake Sakatah in the 1880's stopped in front of the **Giles** house. They were greeted by a large crowd who heard the steamboat's whistle.

The pilot, crew and passengers were invited up town and were shown a lot of hospitality and more! They were given the keys to the town.

Posy and Cozy Inn

Ann and **Ray Weiss** owned a couple of cabins on the south side of lower Lake Sakatah. Knowing **Ann** and **Ray**, I'm sure the guests found the cabins as neat and clean as they look in this photo. The cabins are still standing but are not in use. **Lowell Renken** now owns the property.

It could have been about in this vicinity that the steamboat docked in the 1880's and it departed at a very late hour. Some minor repairs had to be made. The propeller was fouled with weeds. And, some of the passengers were fouled up with some of Waterville's amber fluid. Songs were sung by Sakatah's He Fourettes. The boat arrived at Dingman's bridge at daylight and was out of commission for the time being. The rest of the trip to Morristown was made in a farmer's cattle rack. (notes of boat trip by **Walt Sanborn**)

Molly & Glenn Preuss, Sylvia & Art Roeglin, Grace & Harold Preuss, Harriet & Jack Backman, Carol & Jim Blanchett were in Chicago. (1955)

Greetings From Waterville, Minn.

Deno's

Abolt and **Adeline Deno** owned these cabins for many years. They were located behind **Bob** and **Bea Sherratt's** home on Main Street.

Roland and **Roger**, sons of **Abolt** and **Adeline**, were young boys in 1955. I'll bet they went to see "Lady and the Tramp" that was showing at the beatutiful Gem. They may have even gone with some of the children who were guests in their cabins.

WE MAKE VERY LOW PRICES ON
KITCHEN CABINETS
J. J. WORLEIN & CO.
"The Home Furnishers"

Happenings at Osborn's

Dr. **Seth Osborn** owned this resort on the south side of Lake Tetonka. **Mildred Osborn** lived in the home in recent years—one of Waterville's best bridge players. Both home and cabin are still standing. There were other cabins also that were part of the resort and would be bought later by **Vincent Wilmes** that can be found on page 7-10.

It was along this same part of the lake that my brother and I and our friends would fish bullheads. We would cast our line out with a nightcrawler and slip sinker on the end. The rod would be propped up on a rock and we would wait until the tip of the rod moved and then crank it in. If the fish weren't biting we would walk over to the dam, see the fish trap, talk to the Rausch girls or talk to the tourists about how well the fish were biting last week or go up to **Ward's** to buy a pop. Life was never boring down at **Osborn's**.

The Frank Marzahn's left for their new home in Florida. (1944)

Greetings From Waterville, Minn.

Authenticity

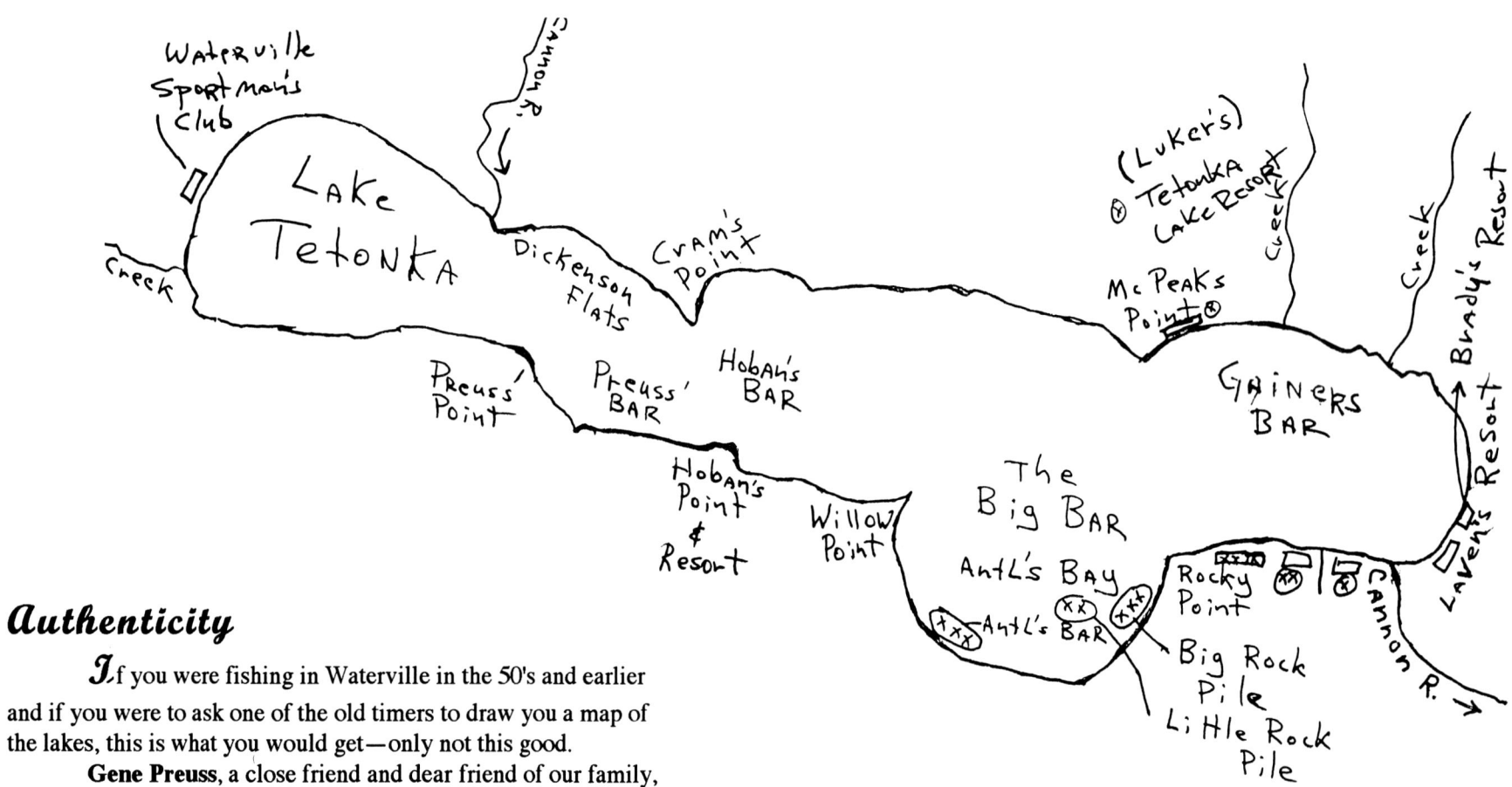

If you were fishing in Waterville in the 50's and earlier and if you were to ask one of the old timers to draw you a map of the lakes, this is what you would get—only not this good.

Gene Preuss, a close friend and dear friend of our family, learned well what his father, **Glenn**, had taught him about the Waterville lakes and how to fish. I told him not to get too fancy with the maps and he drew them just the way his dad would have drawn them.

Picture your dark green metal tackle box filled with Heddon lures, Lazy Ikes, some plastic red and white bobbers. At the bottom of your tackle box, below the bandaid tin containing hooks and under the pliers, is a crumpled map of Lake Tetonka and Lake Sakatah.

Of course, an authentic old timer would not tell you where to go to catch the fish. **Gene Preuss** isn't an old timer but he is authentic. Good fishing!

Thelma Cram, Charlotte Backman and Wendell Holtan received perfect arithmetic papers. (1931)

Page 7-32

Greetings From Waterville, Minn.

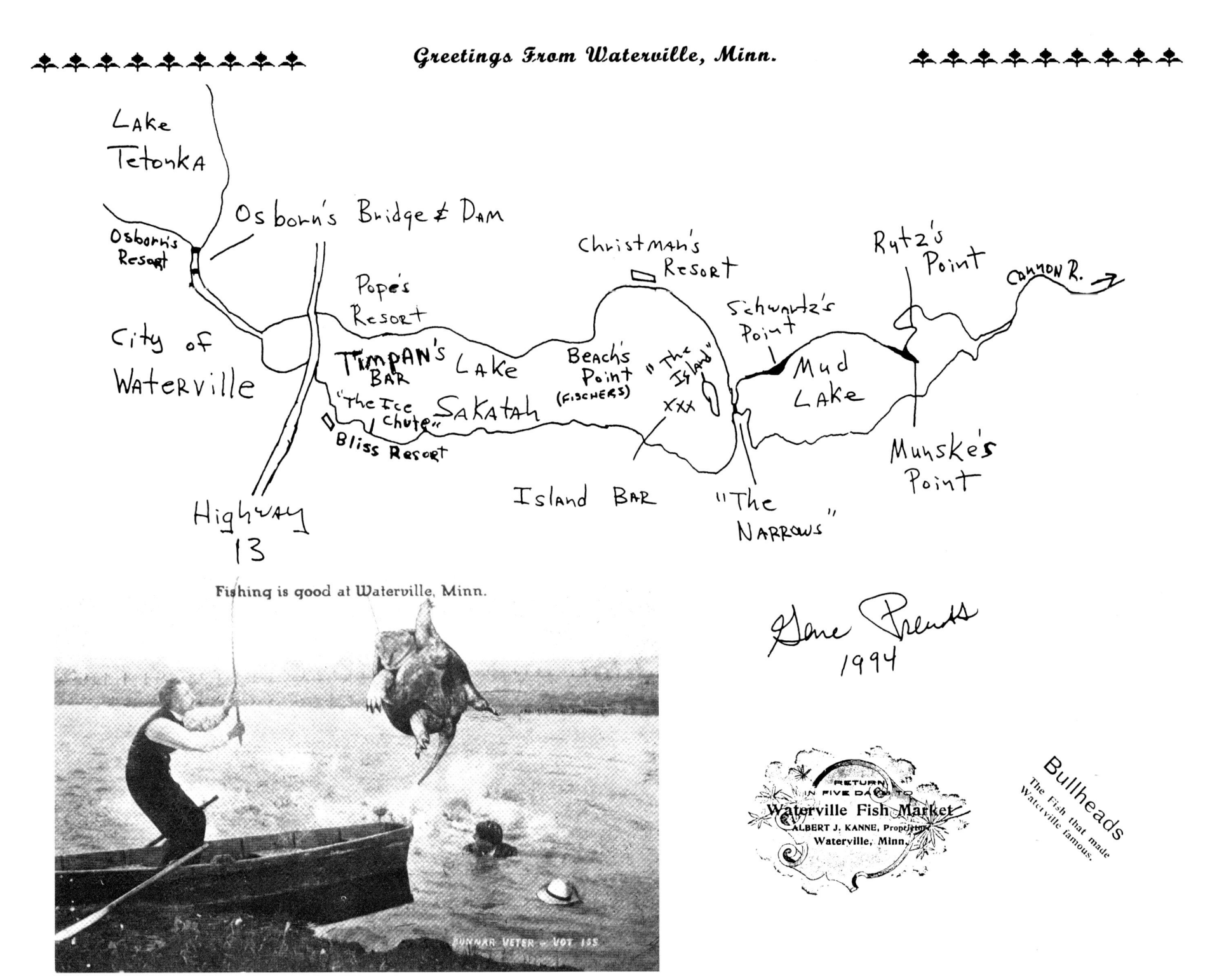

Lake Tetonka
Osborn's Resort
Osborn's Bridge & Dam
Pope's Resort
Christman's Resort
Rutz's Point
Cannon R.
City of Waterville
Timpan's Bar
Lake Sakatah
Beach's Point (Fischers)
"The Island"
xxx
Schwartz's Point
Mud Lake
"The Ice Chute"
Bliss Resort
Munske's Point
Highway 13
Island Bar
"The Narrows"

Fishing is good at Waterville, Minn.

Gene Prents
1994

Waterville Fish Market
ALBERT J. KANNE, Proprietor
Waterville, Minn.

Bullheads
The Fish that made Waterville famous.

G.W. Bluhm and neighbors have raised $1800 for the purpose of extending the county ditch two miles connecting it with the Cannon River. (1910)

Page 7-33

Greetings from Waterville, Minn.

Waterville High School

This has been the home of our education. We have always taken great pride in not only the building, but also in the atmosphere which prevails for young people in quest of knowledge. It is with a feeling of utmost regret that we leave this school to go out into the world. We are confident, however, that regardless of how far away we may find ourselves we shall never forget the many happy school days spent here and we shall always remain loyal to the ideals instilled during our brief sojourn.

(1948 Buccaneer Log)

The school is in the center

The school was the center of the community. Much of what happened in the community centered around what happened in the school.

For every community in Minnesota at the turn of the century, there exists a postcard of their school. When this photo was taken, it shows the newly built school in the middle (1909) and several other new buildings: the Security State Bank (1908), the Post Office, the **George J. Dressel** building (1892) which stands next to the **F.F. Marzahn** building (1895).

The first commencement was in 1883. There were two graduates: **Ida Mae Sheldon** and **Mary Trimbane**. The first superintendent was **L.Z Rogers**.

Waterville was always fortunate in having superintendents that served both the district and the community well. **Herbert Mahler** and **John Kunelius** were two of the best. **Don Bohn**, however, wins the award for dedication. His tenure as an outstanding teacher, administrator and coach, not to mention, as a parent, provided Waterville educators with a great model to emulate.

In 1954 Diane Nelson taught a class above the Citizens State Bank. Bill Walz and Larry Ward were two of her students.

Page 8-1

Greetings from Waterville, Minn.

Waterville's First Teacher

In 1857 the first school was built with **Miss Davison (later Mrs Hitchcock)** serving as Waterville's first teacher. There were 13 pupils.

A stone from the old school that used to sit where the football field is located is dated 1878. This stone, pictured at the left, commemorates the date when Waterville became an organized independent school district.

Schools were also located in West Waterville (1st and 4th grades), 5th and 6th grades were in City Hall and the high school was where the football field is now.

I always felt there was something sacred about playing on the Waterville football field. If you put your ear to the grass you could hear the spirits of former Waterville students whispering to you: "The bullheads can wait, stay in school."

Waterville dedicated its football field in 1939 with a game against St. Peter. The students were asked to register their names at **Luther's** to pick up free tickets. Other wise admission was 25 cents.

West Waterville Schools

Beatrice Hayes and her sister, **Marie Hayes Lindenber,** attended the makeshift classrooms in the houses of the West Waterville schools. The home now occupied by **Dorothy Hruska** was used as well as an L-shaped house behind that and up the hill. **Beatrice's** first grade teacher was a **Mrs. Alexander** who taught her the multiplication tables by singing them.

Bob Stavenau, Jim Miller, David Miller, Jeanine Strom were selected as senior class officers. (1952)

Greetings from Waterville, Minn.

Daily Special
NOON LUNCH — 65c
includes Meat — Potatoes — Salad or Vegetable and Beverage
Hot Beef or Hot Pork Sandwich — 70c
Includes Potatoes — Gravy — Soup — Beverage
ENJOY OUR CELEBRATION
O. K. Cafe
Open 6 a. m. to 2 a. m. Daily

1914 Graduation Class

In the 1880's Waterville Independent District was formed and a $9,000 building was constructed. A graded system was installed with **Professor Hedger** as principal. In 1882 the Waterville township had nine districts. Eight of them had school buildings. In 1915 there was a total pupil population of 494.

From 1914 -1918, students could enroll in a normal course that prepared them for teaching.

The graduation class of 1914 was **Carl Bliss, Ralph Callies, Adolph Dehn, George Chapman, Electa Gish, Carlton Huebl, Ellen Grover, Will Kanuit, Floah Kenny, Ernest Lym, Clarence O'Leary, Paul Schulz, Gladys Wood** and **Gladys Worlein.** The normal school graduates were **Ruth Beardsley, Marie Hale, Grace Hause, Tressa Hamele, Caroline Hermel, Bessie Miller, Edna Rice, Beryl Stafford** and **Blanche Williams.**

Carl Bliss was still thinking about the shutout he pitched last week against Janesville. **Clarence O'Leary** was thinking about his two game winning hits.

This photo shows one of the West Waterville school buildings.

Bob Dusbabek, Harold Grover, Bob Nelson, Keith Taylor, and John Sheehy lettered in football. (1940)

Greetings from Waterville, Minn.

A few of Waterville's former students

*I*n 1904 **Miss Tennison's** West Waterville School class consisted of **Lucy Gray, Frances Umphrey, Jennie Darche, Clarence Hartwick, Calvin Hale, Charlie Backman, Charlie Mar, Mary Farrington, Minnie Farrington, Emma Staples, Edgar Callises, Eva Powers, Addie Giles, Gerturde Larson, Earl Florid, George Gel, Jessie Backman, Amilia Hoffman, Frank Lambert, Fran Hrukisa, Otto Slintz, Eva Schulz, Fannie Vanguilder, Marrgie Known, Wenzela Fenny,** and **Eddie Hucka**. (spellings of these names may be incorrect)

The class picture was a big event in elementary school. Students like to be in the entertainment business. That's my 3rd grade class picture taken in 1950. **Miss Rossow** is the teacher—the only teacher to ever send me to the principal's office. She caught me chewing gum. I guess she didn't realize my dad was on the school board.

My classmates were **Laverne Carlson, Keith Stangler, Mary Roemhildt, Vicky Meyers, Polly Ellingworth, Julie Honken, Diane Preuss, Sharon Chambers** (first row), **Joan Hering,** _____, **Janet Frodl, David Svela, Eugene Calcut, Robert Delaske, John Eggers, Mark Sheehy** (second row), _____, **Sandra Hamele, Faye Wolf, Sandra Bluim, Bob Lamont, Bob Delaske, Clarence Harriman** (third row), **Clara Walz, Sandra Hamele, Bill Rieke, Carolea Courtney, Darwyn Slechta,** (fourth row), **Jeanette Koelzer, Joyce Miller, Joan Ruths, David Rosenau, Jim Hollinger, Dwight Baker, Jerry Groh** (fifth row).

Richard Allen crowns Joan Hering as Homecoming Queen. Janice Bucek crowns John Eggers as Homecoming King. (1960)

Greetings from Waterville, Minn.

My own seat

In 1902 the school board voted to purchase the **Cowles** property to build a new schoolhouse. This 1909 photo of the schoolhouse shows the building they voted to build. Remnants of this building still stand.

Beatrice Hayes Hedges who was in the second grade in 1908 and whose father, **Edward**, was a former city treasurer, says, " I was so happy on that first day to find such modern conveniences as seats of our own, large sunny windows and huge blackboards."

All of the elementary grades were on the first floor and the secondary grades (7-12) were on the second floor. There was one room per grade. There was no special music, art or physical education instruction. Each elementary teacher did their own. And, because they did their own, there were no breaks for them except for lunch. They even took us to the bathroom. Question: When did the teachers go to the bathroom?

Daring classroom stunts

Some of **Beatrice's Hedges' classmates** were **Mary and Eilene Martin, Ellen Dusbabek, Olive Cram, Olive Reynolds, Mayon Rardin, Agatha Slechta, Mildred Reynolds, Blanche Rinehart, Jerry Gish, Kenneth McGruder, Eddie Callahan, Romeo (Hap) Watzek** (who used to get up in the middle of the floor and walk on his hands), **Charley Hancuh, Paul Fanning, Levi Atherton and Mason Marzhan**.

The most daring stunt in my time was when **Keith Stangler** placed a tack on **Guy Kelly's** chair. When **Mr. Kelly** sat on that tack every head was bowed in prayer—prayer that he wouldn't think it was me. **Keith** later confessed.

Mr. Kelly was a favorite teacher and coach. He took a lot of interest in his students and players and wasn't afraid to laugh—unless you placed a tack on his chair.

Notice the bell on the roof of this building. It's the same bell that now sits on the front lawn of the high school.

Gordon Sikes, Mary Sheldon, Irene Miller, Chris Gish, Emily Mc Shane were among others who attended their 25th class reunion. (1954) Page 8-5

Greetings from Waterville, Minn.

Are you in this picture?

If you were in the 7th grade around 1908, you might be in this photo. The kids look rather terrified, don't they? That's what 7th grade did to you in those days when you finally joined the senior high kids.

1st Row: **Virgil Perkins, Dennis O'Leary, Marion Spencer, Fred Powell, Adolf Dehn, Calvin Hale**

2nd Row: **Ellen Grover, Harold Kanne, Art Grover, Carl Bliss, William Kanuit, Jay Beach, Clarence O'Leary, Marie Hale**

3rd Row: **Pat Heveron, Gladys Wood, Walter Krenik, Tom Slechta, Florence Tenney, Clara Ehlert, Ed Kinrod, Roy Reardon**

4th Row: **Clara Bartle, Bertha Hoschka, Ralph Callies, Gladys Cram, Gladys Worlein, Ernie Lym, Daisy Tryon, Carlton Huebl**

5th Row: **Paul Schulz, Regis Feany, Vern Harrison, Ida Kottke, Blanche Riehart, Flo Kenney, Roland Kanne, George Chapman, Electa Gish**

A new place with new faces

In 1953 Waterville had its largest enrollment ever. Superintendent **H.A. Mahler** reported an enrollment of 597. Of these 566 were enrolled in the building at Waterville, 20 in the **Sheehy** school and 11 in the **Hermel** school.

The opening day of the seventh grade was, perhaps, the time when we experienced the most school related stress. We not only went from the first floor to the second floor with the big kids, but our class was significantly larger with the addition of country school kids and the kids coming from Elysian. We just coped the best we could. Janice Bucek, for example, was the only one in the sixth grade in her rural, District 169, school west of Elysian. There were five others in the school. She was the head of her class. When she went on to Waterville the next year, it wasn't easy to get to know new faces, new teachers and a big school.

Many of my former classmates had the same challenge—**Jim Clarke, Ida Mae Hall, Janet** and **Jeanette Lorenz, Alice Melchert, Darlene Muellerleile, Carole Pittman, Mary Prenzlow, Jean Radloff, Jim Roemhildt, Marlene Roemhildt, Verna Roemhildt, Joanne Roessler, Pat Schulz, Bob Seifert, Colleen Sheehy, Shirley Sorgatz, Elaine Sperl, Eddie Stangler, Ralph Tolzman, Maynard Villwock, Ken Wetzel, Larry Willis, Richard Willis** and **Ruth Zellmer.** The family of friends that I had begun with in kindergarten now had almost doubled in size and we had to get along as another family in a new place with new teachers. Just like today, things were not so simple in "those" days either.

Gordon Sikes, Walter Larson, and Howard Anderson are the school bus drivers. (1954)

Greetings from Waterville, Minn.

Music man comes to town

This picture was taken at about the time the new school was built. Left to right in the front row are: **Charles Backman, Roger Preuss, Herman Solyntjes, Glenn Preuss, Betty Aberle** and **Betty Luther.** Second Row: **Doris Clemons, Sylvia Roemhildt, Letty Burick** (director), **Loretta Hebl, Hanley Holtan, John O'Leary, Jack Backman** and **Herbert Kapaun.** Third row: **Ron Taylor, Herb Stowe, Bill Luther, Wendall Holtan, Alvin Miller, Hubert Johnson, Louie Spooner, Edwin Kapaun.** Back row: **Vic Christjaner, Francis Pate** and **Sylvester Pate.**

This was the first high school band. A music man came to town and sold the entire band Singer instruments. He mentioned something about "trouble in river city."

A body under the bridge

To attend the new school from the West end of town, the kids had to cross White Water River bridge. It had waist-high stone walls on each side. A tragedy occurred one cold winter day in the fall as told by **Beatrice Hedges.**

A shy little boy, **Douglas Tenney,** failed to return home from school. His mother and sisters who lived near us were frantic and enlisted the help of everyone to find him. As darkness fell, it was impossible to continue as the streets were poorly lit with kerosene pole lights. As dawn broke, a search began. Then someone discovered his lifeless little frozen body under the bridge. The supposition was that some of the cruel, bigger boys had either forced him to jump or had pushed him over the ledge. There was so much hush-hush about it and I was so young that if the culprits were found and punished—no one ever said.

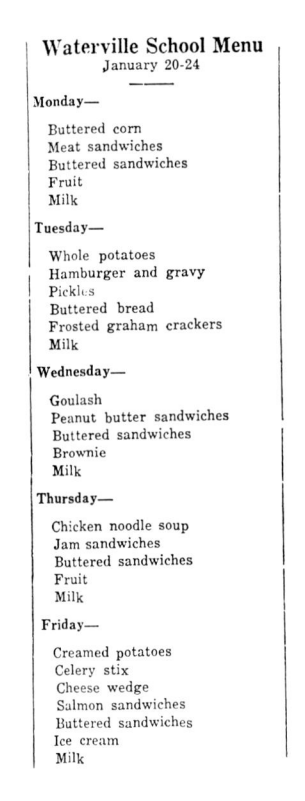

HEADQUARTERS FOR SCHOOL SUPPLIES
STUCKY'S PHARMACY
Waterville, Minnesota

Waterville School Menu
January 20-24

Monday—
Buttered corn
Meat sandwiches
Buttered sandwiches
Fruit
Milk

Tuesday—
Whole potatoes
Hamburger and gravy
Pickles
Buttered bread
Frosted graham crackers
Milk

Wednesday—
Goulash
Peanut butter sandwiches
Buttered sandwiches
Brownie
Milk

Thursday—
Chicken noodle soup
Jam sandwiches
Buttered sandwiches
Fruit
Milk

Friday—
Creamed potatoes
Celery stix
Cheese wedge
Salmon sandwiches
Buttered sandwiches
Ice cream
Milk

Tom Rohrer and Duane Hill are high scorers for the Bucs but they lose to Janesville and New Prague. (1951)

Greetings from Waterville, Minn.

The old gym

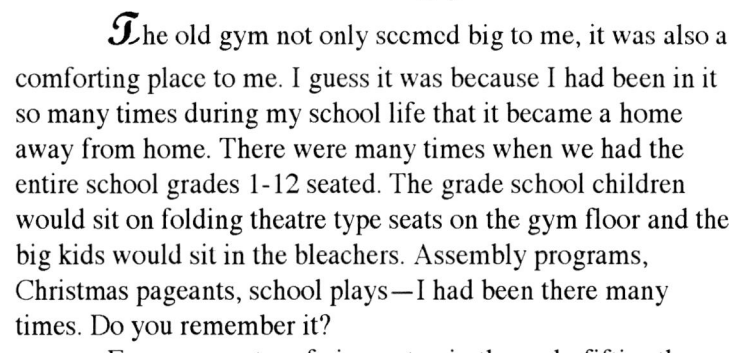

The old gym not only seemed big to me, it was also a comforting place to me. I guess it was because I had been in it so many times during my school life that it became a home away from home. There were many times when we had the entire school grades 1-12 seated. The grade school children would sit on folding theatre type seats on the gym floor and the big kids would sit in the bleachers. Assembly programs, Christmas pageants, school plays—I had been there many times. Do you remember it?

For a youngster of nine or ten in the early fifties the "old gym" did seem like the Target Center of the south. Sitting on the balcony floor and leaning over the wall to see **Ron** and **Don Swift** play basketball was great entertainment. **Mr. Harold Hebel's** band would be in one corner of the gym during halftime. We would stand to sing the school song.

From the shores of Lake Sakatah,
Raise the cry of Victory!
Let us wage a sportsman's battle;
Fight with courage gallantly.
Admiration and our praises,
Call for songs of loudest cheer,
For we glory in the record,
Of the Valiant Buccaneers!

Sitting on the floor next to the edge of the balcony the spectators would step over us as we watched the show below. It's a wonder no one ever fell over the balcony. My dream that one day I would be down there playing basketball did come true. By that time I had grown, the gym had shrunk to become one of the smallest in the state. For me, it still was the best.

It was officially dedicated on November 11 in 1932.

The new old high school

"On Friday, November 11, 1932, the new high school building and auditorium will be dedicated with an appropriate program," reads the Waterville *Advance* of 1932. **Mr. R.R. Reeder** was superintendent and **Mr. B.C. Graff** was president of the school board. For many Watervillians, their good ol' school days happened in this building. To be chauffeured in **Robert Bittrich's** '36 Chevy was the highlight of my elementary school days.

Northern States Power repaired the wire in this photo. Employees at that time (1944) were **Chick Reynolds, Earl Peterson, Joe Kutzma, Ike Bartlet, John Poehler, Bill Stucky,** and **Leonard Nelson. Reynolds** and **Peterson** were linemen and may be the ones in the photo. **Bob Kerr** worked briefly in 1941, went to serve in the war and returned to work at NSP from 1945-1982.

No doubt some kids wanted to delay the opening of school by tampering with the wires.

HARDEGGER'S LAKE JEFFERSON
—DANCE TO—
SPIKE HASWELL
Jolly Millers
SATURDAY, SEPT. 8
Eddie Wilfhart
SUNDAY, SEPT. 9

School board members in 1939 were Tony Stucky, H.T. Stowe, Clemons, Slechta, W.S. Farrington, and William Luther.

Greetings from Waterville, Minn.

Study hall was for visiting

The row of windows in the upper right of the card to the left belonged to the study hall room. It held maybe sixty to eighty students. The whole idea behind study hall was to see how much visiting you could do while making it appear as if you were studying.

The best part of study hall for me was to go into **Miss Bishop's** library (and it was her library) to check out a *Sports Afield* or *Field & Stream* magazine.

The new school with the new cafeteria and elementary wing was completed in 1957. High school teachers that year were **Wallace Lymburn (principal), Tom Abbott, Elizabeth Bishop, Don Bohn, Ernest Dahl, Meredith Kelley, Blanche Kindstrom, Larry Meskan, June Sautbine, Patricia Bany, George Barnard, Tom Bengston, Robert Butler, Maurice Enghausen, Herman Winkels, Joan Gardner,** and **Don Hopke.**

Waterville's heroes

Big school news in 1958 was that Waterville was leaving the District 13 Conference and would join the Gopher Conference. People were saying we should have done it a few years earlier when we had the **Swift** boys playing and **Doug Grover** and **Ralph Kaupa**.

I was fortunate to have attended a K-12 school where all of the kids were in one building. The older kids became your heroes and role models. The **Bittrich's, Grover's, Swift's, Kaupa's,** and **Tommy Roher** and other students older than you had as much to do with shaping one's behavior as did your teachers and parents.

Dennis Grover was in double figures, **Bill Norman** had nine points and **Bill Tolzman** had eight rebounds in a 1958 loss to Le Center.

Amy Luker, Willard Williams, Eugene Clemons, Roger Eggers, Ella Morganweck, Marilyn Pope and Ben Kniefel star in "The Sunshine Twins." (1945)   Page 8-9

Watervillians:

Where all of the women are gentle, where all of the men are helpful and all of the children think they are well above average

Some of Waterville's WWI Soldiers

They said WWI was the "war to end all wars." American foot soldier were called "doughboys" and endured the war from 1914-1918.

The headlines in the Friday, July 3, 1914 *Sentinel* read, *Archduke and wife victims of assasins: Heir to throne of Austria and his consort are murdered in Bosnia.* As much as America tried to remain neutral, it could not. As a result of an incident in a country far away from Waterville, Waterville would send its sons to fight. The world would never be the same again.

The soldier on the right is **Walter Bartelt**, center, **Percy Mack**, **Wencil Knish**. The three left together for the service. Did they return?

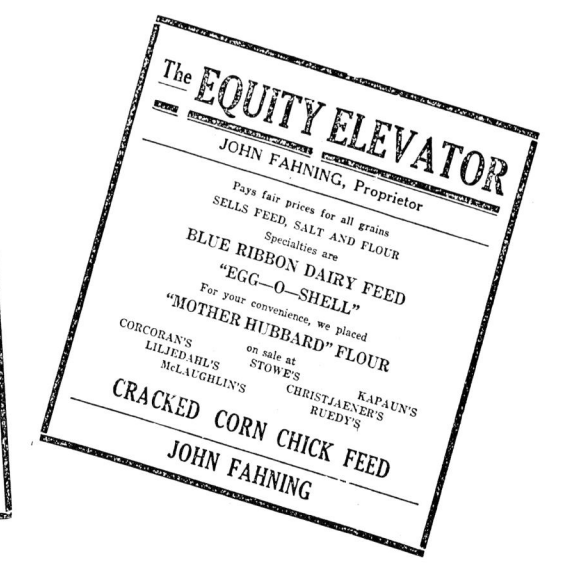

Coal and a tragic death

If your coal bin was empty in 1918, this is how it was filled. "Telephone #10 and it will be filled with high grade coal. Fahning and Lampert." It's November of 1918 and it must be cold. The lady has a scarf wrapped around her head and she wants the best coal deal **John** can give her.

John Fahning (on the far right) came to America from Germany as a boy in 1872. He became an early leader in the community and married **Caroline Peterson** in 1897. Four children were born: **Grace, John, Paul, and Clara. John Fahning, Jr's.** tragic death on September 11, 1915 was a shock to all.

With his younger brother, **Paul**, they started out hunting on a Saturday afternoon. They walked the south shore of Lake Sakatah to Babcock's Point where they spotted a woodcock. **Paul** shot at the animal but missed. **John** cocked his gun to take a shot, but his dog, that was chained to his belt got tangled in the chain and he laid his gun down. In recovering the gun, the gun discharged.

John, Jr. was a sophomore in the Waterville High School and was a bright, popular boy, a real favorite with his friends. It was reported that his sad fate cast a spell of gloom over the whole community.

John Fahning was made a partner in the Lampert Lumber Company's office at Waterville in 1897. He was regarded as one of the leading lumber men in this section of the state. His family occupied a high position in the social life of the town and were held in high esteem. He sold his business to his son **Paul** in 1935. He also operated a grain elevator selling out to the Commander Elevator Co.

John Fahning died on February 24, 1943 while shoveling snow. At his funeral **Mr. William Christ-Janer** sang two solos and was accompanied on the organ by **Mrs. Hugo Antl**.

Paul Fahning sold the business to **D.T. Palmer** in 1955.

H.W. Wendelschfer delivered a new Ford to Henry Kading yesterday. (1914)

Page 9-2

Greetings from Waterville, Minn.

Charles Glotfelter

Charles Glotfelter came to Waterville in 1886 having accepted a position as manager of the Waterville Furniture Factory. He was at this position for 13 years. He then returned to agricultural life and took up a specialty, the raising of high-grade Shorthorn cattle and Shropshire sheep. In 1916 he was considered to be one of the leading live-stock men of the state and vicinity.

In 1881 he married a **Hattie Potter**. They had one child, **June**, who later became **Mrs. Christman**. In 1890 he married for a second time to **Florence Rogers**, a daughter of **L.Z. Rogers**. They had three children, **Helen, George,** and **Laura**. He became a representative in the Minnesota State Legislature in 1907. In 1908 he organized the Security State Bank of which he became president.

"The Shorthorn Breeders' Association of Minnesota will hold their annual meeting at Waterville on June 17," read the *Waterville Sentinel* of 1914. **C.W. Glotfelter** is in charge of the committee.

Waterville's Unsung Heroes

The first meeting of the Waterville Fire Department was held in 1884. Some of the former fire chiefs in order are: **D. E. Potter, CW Glotfelter, Julius Worlein, W.J. Kalow, W. G. Gish, Frank Dusbabek, Al Fredell, Glenn Preuss, Jack Salzle, Jerome Janda, Elmer Stangler.** In 1957 Waterville's fire department had 20 members. Nine of them are shown in this photo: Chief **Erv Schwichtenberg, Art Roeglin, Don Coon, Jerome Janda, Al Fredell, Elmer Dusbabek, Robert Sherratt,** and **Robert Krause.** Also, **Jack Salzle, Howard Coon, Robert Kerr, Bob Dusbabek, Glenn Preuss, Fred Hrdlichka, Art Bartelt, Dick Kirchner, Robert Rausch, Bob Connors,** and **Ken Kletschka.** The photo was taken in front of City Hall and the fire station on Second Street.

Mayor Aberle has declared all pinball machines to be out of order. John Weaver will enforce the order. (1946)

Greetings from Waterville, Minn.

The Three Store System

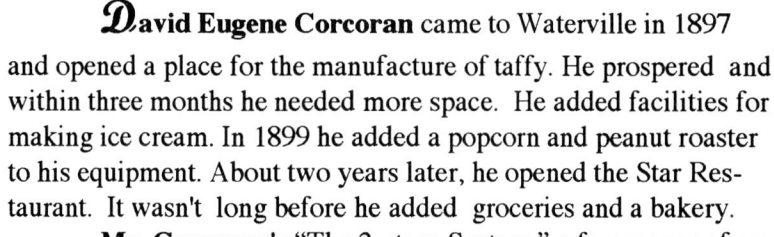

David Eugene Corcoran came to Waterville in 1897 and opened a place for the manufacture of taffy. He prospered and within three months he needed more space. He added facilities for making ice cream. In 1899 he added a popcorn and peanut roaster to his equipment. About two years later, he opened the Star Restaurant. It wasn't long before he added groceries and a bakery.

Mr. Corcoran's "The 3-store System," a forerunner of our mini-malls, enabled him to become one of the successful merchants and manufacturers of Waterville. In 1898 he married **Carrie Oradson** of St James. They had three children: **Mamie, Irene,** and **Russell** (who died at the age of 13 in 1913).

The photo shows **Dave** with the cigar. **Ed Courtney**, who will eventually manage the store, is to **Dave's** right and **William Nierenz** is at the counter.

In the 1900's, workers in the restaurant were **David Corcoran, Caroline Corcoran, Nora Sanford,** and **May Straub**. **David Corcoran** put in the "the first white way" (i.e. street lights) in Waterville. An innovator and entrepreneur, **Dave** would be proud to know that one of his oak restaurant tables with the white marble top would hold a Macintosh computer on which a history of Waterville would be written.

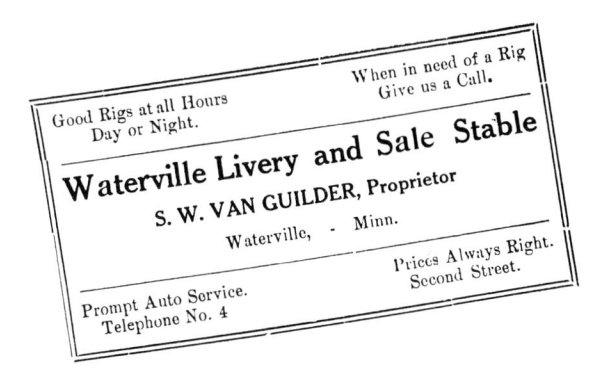

Waterville Livery and Sale Stable
Good Rigs at all Hours Day or Night.
When in need of a Rig Give us a Call.
S. W. VAN GUILDER, Proprietor
Waterville, - Minn.
Prompt Auto Service.
Telephone No. 4
Prices Always Right.
Second Street.

Proprietor of Waterville's
THREE STORE SYSTEM

ON SATURDAY ONLY

WE WILL SELL

Oatmeal, per package . . **8c**
Toasted Cream of Rye . . **5c**
Corn Flakes **5c**
E-C Corn Flakes . . . **5c**
Puffed Wheat **8c**
Puffed Rice **12c**

These prices are good for Saturday only, terms spot cash and take all you can carry away. We pay cash for everything, including Eggs. Bring in your cackleberries.

D. CORCORAN   "He Treats You Right"

On sale at Corcoran's Three Store System in 1914: bulk raisins at 10 cents per pound.

Greetings from Waterville, Minn.

The Waterville Citizen's Band

Well I see **Bill Luther** holding his clarinet in "The Waterville Citizen's Band." He's probably wishing the picture taking session would be over so the band could play another number. It was nice that someone recognized the contribution this band had made to those early years in Waterville's history.

Well, **Bill**, you and the other band members have been officially enshrined as part of Waterville's history. Play us a tune as we march through Waterville's history.

Members of this turn-of-the-century band included **Joe Tuschek** (trombone), **Fred Koette** (baritone), **Bill Luther** (clarinet), **Frank Schmidt** (baritone), **Theodore Stavenau** (bass horn), **Charley Quiram's** father, **Ernie Williams, Joseph Giles, Louis Morshing, Charlie Quiram, Arnold Callies, Arthur Zellmer, Otto Roeglin** (bass drum).

Break time at the Waterville Furniture Factory

Some of the workers were **Carl Stavenau, Bill Haase, Martin Atherton, Ernie Chambers, Ben Atherton,** and **Ole Gronseth.**

"Old" **Bill Haase** ran the factory at one time. It was still standing as recently as 1950 as pictured on a Backman Produce Company calendar of Waterville. The factory was located on the corner of 1st Street and Lake Street, where the Waterville Health Care Center is currently located.

Thanks to **Bob Dusbabek**, I have a 1916-1917 Waterville Furniture Co. Catalogue. An oak secretary sells for $11.00. How many would you like?

Another furniture factory was built in 1866 by **Todd** and **Louth** on Third Street. **Wick Beach** was hired at a salary of ten cents a day to ride a horse to power the turning lathe.

Don Werner and Kenyon Cram are the first farmers to bring spring wheat to the local GTA Elevator. (1966)

Greetings from Waterville, Minn.

Game of catch?

When I was hit by a baseball pitched by **Doug Grover** I switched to track and field. I didn't have to worry about ducking when running the long jump. The young men in this 1909 photo didn't have the option. It was either baseball or bullheads. I'm glad they chose baseball. They started a rich tradition in Waterville that exists today.

Pictured in this photo to the left are **Mr. Chapman, Mr. Tallard, Pete Kuaak, Bruce Stone, Harry Stangler, Bill Farrington, Dan Hartwick, Oscar Fricke, Charles Luther,** and **Bill Luther.**

Waterville's "Babe Ruths"

Baseball in Waterville was less than 25 years old when this photo was taken in the early 1900's. The names on the reverse side of this photo on the right read: (back row) **Walter Denny, Roy Jargo, Emmit Smith, Ed Jargo, Banty Fowler, Oscar Finke, Ben Atherton;** (middle row) **Shorty Stone** in the middle and the other two were unknown, (front row) **Bill Atherton**, and **Nelson**.

In 1914 Waterville beat Le Sueur Center by a score of 9 to 3. "**Lee** for Waterville demonstrated that he is some pitcher and whenever he had men on bases he steamed up and invariably got the next batter on strikes."

Tetonka Aces defeat Iosoco Wildcats. Star players were Arlie Christjaner and Don Hoban. (1940)

Greetings from Waterville, Minn.

Mrs. Bert Ryan and Mort Mengis

*T*his photo was taken in 1929. **Mrs. Bert Ryan**, wife of the photographer, and **Mort Mengis**, mail carrier, are standing on the steps. I'm not exactly certain where in Waterville this was taken. Do you know?

Mort lived in West Waterville on the corner of Lake and Cottrill. He had a picket fence surrounding his place. In his back yard was enough split wood to last a decade. Chopping and splitting wood and walking his mail route kept **Mort** in pretty good shape.

Luther's Workers

*L*uther's Ben Franklin was Waterville's Mall of America. In the photo are **Bill Luther, Jack Luther** is kneeling, **Hazel Fowler, Minnie Van Fleet, Mabel Morshing, Ruth Eggers,** and **Addie Spooner**.

A 1931 **Luther's** Cash Store ad read, "Wheat isn't the only thing that's gone down." They advertised Boys' Knee Pants for 98 cents, Boys' Bow Ties for 10 cents, Boys' Leather Belts for 25 cents, and Rayon Berets for 25 cents.

Luther's store was on the north side of Main Street at one time. It was truly a family run business. **Bill** worked for his father, **Charles** and later **Bill's** sons, **Bill Jr.** and **Jack** worked for their father. Mrs. **Bill Luther** also worked in the store.

I know one of the saddest moments in our lives occurred when **Bill Luther** junior died—a decorated World War II veteran. He was a close friend of my parents and he enjoyed eating ice cream with them. I remember **Bill** as being a very nice person as were all of the **Luther's**. No doubt this is why they had one of Waterville's most successful businesses for many years.

The Gus Bluhm farm home in Cannoville was destroyed by fire. (1916)

Greetings from Waterville, Minn.

This is a stick-up!

In 1916 the First National Bank in Waterville had a capital, surplus and profits of about $40,000. Its president was **F.H. Wellcome** and **Geo. E. Greene** was Vice President. The man in the vest in the photo is assistant cashier, **Pat Drews**. The other man is cashier, **Al Robson**.

In 1952 both **Al** and **Pat** and my father and **Phyllis Stavenau** spent some time in the vault (seen behind **Al Robson**) together. It seems on a quiet Monday afternoon on August 18 in 1952 a short man wearing a straw hat and carrying two shoe boxes and a sawed-off shotgun held up the Citizens State Bank (formerly known as the First National Bank).

He ordered my father, **Edgar Eggers**, to clean out the cash drawers and then herded the four of them into the vault. The "shoe box bandit" as he was later to be called in *Detective Magazine*, left with $4,800 and, in his panic, dropped $2,500 on the sidewalk.

Fred Hrdlicka of the Security State Bank was one of the first to discover the robbery. The four trapped bank employees were able to escape due to a safety catch on the inside. The bank robber was eventually captured and died in prison. As one teen-age girl said who was quoted in the *Minneapolis Morning Tribune*, "Nothing ever like this happened in Waterville." I guess she never heard about Jesse James camping out on Klondike Hill.

Bandit Robs Waterville Bank of $2,360, Flees Southwest

Minneapolis Tribune photo by Earl Seubert
BANK CASHIER RE-ENACTS STICKUP SCENE
F. A. Drews puts up hands as deputy 'points gun'

CITIZENS STATE BANK, SCENE OF WATERVILLE, MINN., ROBBERY
Lone bandit sped away with $2,360, dropped $2,500 on sidewalk

Louie Grassinger brings Clellan Card to Waterville for Bullhead Days. (1964)

Greetings from Waterville, Minn.

If you could talk to them, what would you say?

Ben Atherton, John Fierny, Cal Hale, Bill Atherton and John Smith were members of Waterville's baseball team in this early 1900's photo. As you look into the faces of these five ball players, what do you think they might say to you? It would probably be something like, "So, you're from Waterville? How are things? Do they still play baseball there?"

Are they just getting ready to play or have they just finished playing? Their clothes aren't too dirty so I think they're waiting for the other players to arrive and someone said, "Hey, how about a picture?"

There's a look of uncertainty in their faces. Maybe Morristown is coming to town.

Cannonville Band in Waterville

News from Cannonville in March of 1914: A fine boy arrived at the home of **Mr. and Mrs Henry Rosenau** on the 10th. **Miss Marjorie Schubel** held a basket social last Friday evening. A nice crowd attended. Games were played and the baskets were sold at a reasonable price.

Cannonville was located north of Waterville in the vicinity of Cannonville Lutheran Church. When this 1909 photo was taken, its band rivaled that of neighboring cities like Waterville. I suppose this occasion was a street fair and parade—maybe even Decoration Day.

The members of the Cannonville Band at this time were: **Otto Roeglin** (snare drum), **Ben Bluhm** (base drum), **Quiram** (Tuba), **Charles Roemhildt** (Baritone), **August Roeglin** (trombone), **Gust Quiram** (trombone), **Rud Zellmer** (piccolo), **Edgar Morsching** (trumpet), **John Gesch** (trumpet), **Art Zellmer** (trumpet), **Louis Morsching** (trumpet).

Last week **Miss Cecila Roemhildt** visited with her sister, Mrs. **Art Zellmer**. Do you suppose **Art** played a solo for them?

Dr. J. Dunnwald has taken over the veterinary practice of Dr. Seth Osborn. (1946)

Greetings from Waterville, Minn.

Fresh meat for sale at Comstock's Market

Mr. **Frank Comstock** and son, **Lester**, helped make Waterville famous for its meat markets. **Comstock's** Market was located where the **Dean Thrun** Insurance Agency is now located. **Darlene Comstock Thrun** is the daughter of **Lester**.

Frank started in the meat business in the late 1920's. His first location was on the west side of where **Stucky's** Pharmacy was located. The building has since burned. **Frank** died in about 1944. **Lester** and **Phyllis** took over and operated **Comstock's** Market until the mid 1960's.

In 1961 **Lester** and **Phyllis** probably heard their customers talk much about the recent move of **John Nelson** into the old Gem Theatre building. Waterville merchants were happy to see that well built building put to good use.

Expecting a busy day at Comstocks

Frank Comstock and his mother, **Minnie**, are expecting a busy day in their market in 1948. They have expanded their meat business to include a few groceries. I wonder if **Lester's** father, **Frank**, shot that big buck hanging on the wall or if **Lester** did?

You can buy a six pack of Coke for 25 cents.

The war has been over for a few years but Waterville is still giving "air raid warning signal" warnings. If you want to get more information about how to survive an atomic attack, you can write to the Department of Documents in Washington. Without a six pack of Coke, who would want to?

Irene Wilcox has a nice recipe for Easy White Frosting in her *You Name It* column. (1964)

Greetings from Waterville, Minn.

J.J. Dawald

There were two meat markets in the 1880's. **Botz** and **Tidball** owned one and the other was managed by **P. Rice**. They carried a full line of fresh and salted meats.

Jacob Dawald owned one of Waterville's first hotels: The Waterville House. **Jacob Dawald** had a son, **John**, who became known for his meat market. His market was located on the north side of Main Street in what later would become the OK Cafe.

In this picture, **Lawrence Bowman** is on the left, **John J. Dawald** is in the middle and **Howard Dawald** is on the right. Their meat market featured the first refrigerated cases in Waterville. The picture was taken in 1922.

Through wind, sleet, hail . . .

There weren't too many days when you didn't run into **Jim Hruska** and **Mort Mengis**—I mean, literally run into them. They would visit every house in Waterville twice a day during the days when there were two deliveries—morning and afternoon. They would carry up to 70 pounds of paper and walk their routes. They were power walking long before it became a fad.

In the 1950's **Hiller Teff** and **Ernest Lillienskoild** were the two rural carriers. **Linden Ebling, Harold Rickard,** and **Al Koelzer** worked in the main post office on the corner of Main and Third Street.

I liked to go into the post office and check the "most wanted" bulletin board. It helped me feel that Waterville was doing its part to help J. Edgar Hoover.

Pictured in this photo are: (back row) **Linden Ebling, Al Koelzer, Jim Hruska, Ernie Lillienskoild.** (front row) **Harold Rickard, Mort Mengis, Hiller Teff.**

Clarence Bohlen has brood sows for sale. Telephone 1F3. (1951)

Greetings from Waterville, Minn.

Ready for the airships

The Waterville banner is ready, the guy has his girl (or wife), the parade is about to start, he's driving a new car, the weather is cooperating, it's going to be a great day to celebrate the Fourth of July in 1914.

After the parade he and his mate will drive to Madison Lake where the Waterville band is providing music for their celebration. A large crowd is expected.

A big drawing card in Madison Lake will be the airship flights. This will be the first time they will have seen an airship.

Do you know who "they" are?

Waterville's music men

They are a classy looking bunch, don't you think? Waterville has a tradition of music and bands. In this 1940's photo, the tradition is being kept alive.

From left to right are **Pete Solyntjes, Charles Roemhildt, William Christjaner, Mr. Knish, Hiller Teff, Al Koelzer, Lawrence Bosacker,** (drummers are not known). The person kneeling is **Tom Slechta**.

They are having a good time. People in Waterville always had a good time when the band was playing.

The 1957 Chevy stolen from Mr. and Mrs. Lloyd Holling was recovered in South Dakota. (1961)

Greetings from Waterville, Minn.

More facts about Waterville citizens you may not know but you wish that you did.

Marlowe Burns: From 1945 to 1974, Marlowe caught 107 walleyes between 9-12 pounds.

Arthur Clark Dehn: Arthur operated a general store here for many years and grew up in Waterville in the old **Dehn** home next to the Commercial Hotel. Most of his life he fished and did carpentry work in the summer and he hunted and trapped in the winter. In later years he had a cottage business on Lake Tetonka. He recalled one time when some neighboring friendly Indians saved him and his family from some warring Indians. In 1943 **Mr.** and **Mrs. Dehn** celebrated their 50th wedding anniversary which was written up in *Life* magazine on July 6. Two weeks before the appearance of the article, **Mrs. Dehn** died. **Arthur** is the father of the painter **Adolph Dehn.**

Anna Dickie: **Anna** was the first woman to run for the U.S. Senate as a major party candidate in 1922.

Electa Gish and **Agatha Coughlin** played for the silent movies. They played in what is now the **Jacobson** building or **Joseph Kapoun** building.

Dr. Herb Huffington memorial library in Kansas is dedicated to the family physician. **Dr. Huffington** served in Waterville in the 50's and 60's. He was respected nationally among family physicians having served as their president for several years. His office was located on 2nd Street south of City Hall and the fire department.

Lucille Krause was the superintendent's secretary for 42 years. She was also the 1944 Waterville Salutatorian.

Glenn Preuss: Few people could equal Glenn's ability to smoke carp. He passed his talent on to his son **Gene**.

Jack Sikel used to give people boat rides in 1915. His boat would dock where the post office is now. It weighed 5000 pounds and held 20 people.

Cut-Nose (Waarpekute Indian): Cut-Nose operated a ferry at the Narrows until a bridge was built. He was one of 38 Indians hung at Mankato in 1862. The order to hang the 38 was given by President Lincoln. His body was exhumed by Dr. Mayo and is now part of the medical exhibit at Mayo Museum in Rochester.

Henry Long Gish: Served in the Minnesota House of Representatives in 1876. He introduced the bill to locate LeSueur County Seat at LeSueur Center

Jessie James Gang : Many claim they made frequent visits to Waterville, posing as fur buyers or lumber dealers. They stopped at Waterville on the way to an attempted Northfield bank robbery, September of 1876. Legend has it that after the bank robbery, he rested on Klondike or Jesse James hill near Elysian.

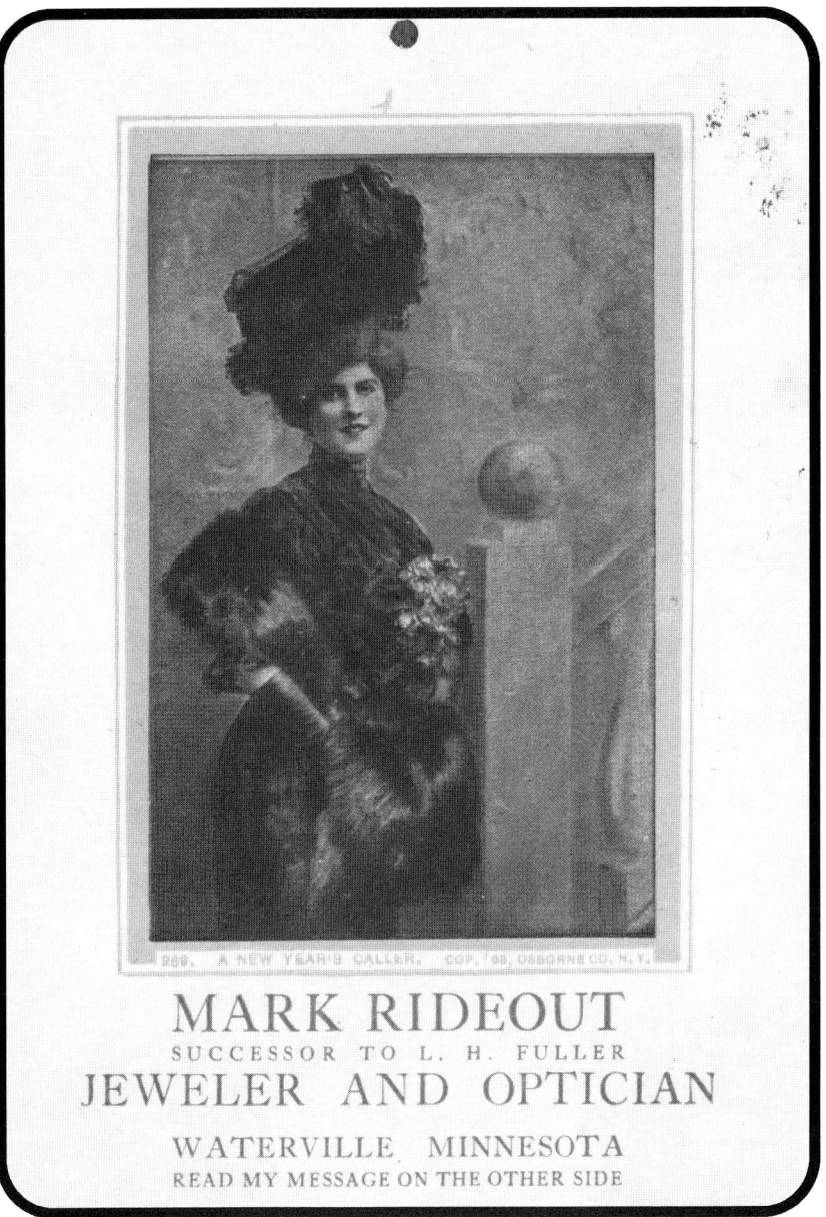

MARK RIDEOUT
SUCCESSOR TO L. H. FULLER
JEWELER AND OPTICIAN
WATERVILLE MINNESOTA
READ MY MESSAGE ON THE OTHER SIDE

George Dusbabek sold his farm to Alvin Rosenau. (1940)

Greetings from Waterville, Minn.

Harold Dressel, Fred Clemons, and **Fred Beese** were the last three members and veterans of WWI. They met for the last time on October 19, 1982.

Roger Preuss designed the federal duck stamp in 1949.

Mrs. Charles Rohl: (**Jim's** mother) was the first in town to bob womens' hair.

Don Bohn first taught industrial arts and boys' physical education when he came to Waterville in 1935. Don was a graduate of Winona and taught first in Bird Island. His daughter, **Nancy**, taught in Japan for many years.

Stu Mann writing for *Minnesota Outdoors* commenting on the Waterville Centennial in 1957 said, "This area has a bright future. The young men who handled the centennial have great civic pride. **Al Werner, Tom Abbott, Harold Preuss, Woody Palmer** and the others have their eyes wide open as to the possibilities of this area with its beautiful lakes and fertile farm lands. And because of the work of this fine group of Minnesotans, many more vacationists will head for this section of the state."

Carl Petersen served as scoutmaster in the 1930's when the troop owned a cabin on Highway 60 between Morristown and Waterville.

Olivia Dehn, sister of artist, **Adolph Dehn**, was also a talented commercial artist.

F.S. Luker had dances at the pavilion located on the east side of Lake Tetonka as early as 1886.

William Stucky captured someone robbing **Mike Folsom's** Bar during the Waterville Centennial in 1957. The same man also robbed **Fahning** Supply, the depot and Waterville Seed and Feed.

Ben Kneifel, Leo Watzek, Donald Solyntjes, Mayland Grubish, Merle Grubish, Francis Janda, Melvin Schulz and **Jerome Janda** left for Camp Rucker on January 22, 1951 for their National Guard training.

The **Louis Grassinger** and **Walter Bittrich** seining crew hauled in 90,000 pounds of rough fish from Lake Elysian in January of 1951. The fish were brought to Lake Sakatah and put in cribs to await shipment.

Wm. Luther, Cleve Cram, James Balfe, Charles Grubbish and **Wm Nadeau** were pallbearers for **Catherine Lawless** who died July 8, 1956. Mrs. Lawless was wife of **James S. Lawless** who operated a second hand store in the "Lawless Brick Block" building now occupied by The Attic run by **Curt Wetzel** and **Lori Stangler**.

Craig Eggers and **Leon Mager** attended the Boy Scout Jamboree at Valley Forge in 1956.

In 1931 the following students had perfect attendance in first grade: **Mary Ellen Griebnow, Melvin Kletschka, Harold Mack, Jr., Mabel Schwartz,** and **Roland Zimbrick**.

George Weaver was busy hauling stone in 1886 for the foundation of **Mr. Everett's** new bank building (that would be the former Security State Bank on the corner of 2nd Street and Main Street).

The men responsible for organizing the 1909 Firemen's Ball are **Will Southwick, Ira Huftellen, Louis Dusbabek, Dan McGovern, Louis Grassinger, Charles Dusbabek, Charles Christman, JJ Worlein, Ed Bleedorn, Chub VanGuilder, Wencel Hancuh, Sam VanGuilder, Charles Dawald, Ed Peterson, J.S. Lawless, Charles Darche,** and **George Spires**.

Joe Lauer won the Christmas lighting contest. (1961)

Greetings from Waterville, Minn.

Ed Courtney died in 1957 at the age of 56. All businesses were asked to close during the the time of the service. He was associated in business with his father-in-law, **Dave Corcoran**. His wife is **Irene Courtney** and their daughters are **Darlene** (operator of the Waterville popcorn wagon), **Arvilla** and **Carollea**.

The WHS graduation class of 1914 was: **Carl Bliss, Ralph Callies, George Chapman, Adolf Dehn, Electa Gish, Ellen Grover, Carlton Huebl, William Kanuit, Flo Kenney, Ernie Lym, Clarence O'Leary, Paul Schulz, Gladys Wood, Gladys Worlein, Mary Ellen Griebnow, Melvin Kletschka, Harold Mack, Jr., Mabel Schwartz,** and **Roland Zimbrick.**

In 1895 the Waterville brass band was on hand to welcome home newly married **George Fuller** and **Nora Hoban.** They were married by Judge **Charles Dolan** at the home of **Nora's** parents, **Mr.** and **Mrs. Steve Hoban** on Thanksgiving Day.

Lewis and **Hannah Stowe** came to Minnesota in 1856. They claimed 160 acres south of town and became one of Waterville's first successful farmers. **Lewis** was elected to the Minnesota legislature in 1872. He served as the Indian Agent on the White Earth Reservation from 1873-1878. He returned to Waterville in 1878. His son **H.H. Stowe** managed a "quality store" on the east side of First National Bank that would later be operated by the **Preuss** brothers and then **Al Werner** and **Bob Buckmaster**. **Lewis** and **Hannah Stowe** are featured in a book entitled *Northern Lights Going to the Sources* by Stephen Sandell. It is used in today's schools to study Minnesota history.

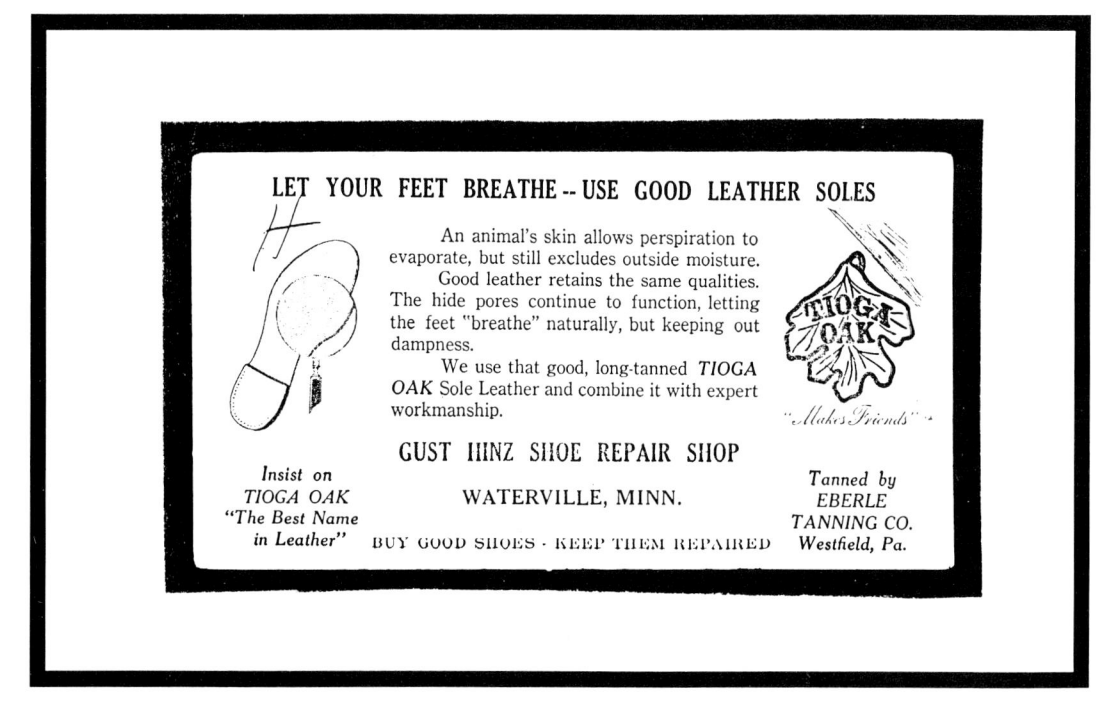

H.H. STOWE "QUALITY STORE"

Boys! School is nearly out. You have until Saturday, June to get the Auto. Get busy now and ride! Come in and see me.

Strawberries Are Fine and Cheap!
Large "dry" quarts (at market) now 15c

A Snap in Assorted Preserves!
(in glass) regular 25c.; finest goods, at 20c.

Fancy Dry Logan Berries Regular 40c.; at . . 35c

LET YOUR FEET BREATHE -- USE GOOD LEATHER SOLES

An animal's skin allows perspiration to evaporate, but still excludes outside moisture. Good leather retains the same qualities. The hide pores continue to function, letting the feet "breathe" naturally, but keeping out dampness.

We use that good, long-tanned TIOGA OAK Sole Leather and combine it with expert workmanship.

GUST HINZ SHOE REPAIR SHOP

WATERVILLE, MINN.

BUY GOOD SHOES - KEEP THEM REPAIRED

Insist on TIOGA OAK "The Best Name in Leather"

TIOGA OAK "Makes Friends"

Tanned by EBERLE TANNING CO. Westfield, Pa.

Dr. Ralph Buesgens came to Waterville in 1950 and never left. He knows more about the people of Waterville than any other person. When I tripped in a Montgomery track meet and got a knee full of cinders, **Dr. Buesgens** and his wife cleaned them out. **Dr. Buesgens** left in a few just to remind me to walk the straight and narrow. Waterville struck gold when **Buesgens** and **Huffington** came to town. It's one thing to be good at what you do but to be respected and good is quite an accomplishment.

Dr. Ralph Buesgens is honored for 45 years as general practitioner in Waterville. (1995)

Greetings from Waterville, Minn.

Telephone talk about bullheads

Street fairs to celebrate the Fourth of July have become a Waterville ritual in 1889. The Waterville Band is marching east on Main Street past the Commercial Hotel and the City Livery that will eventually be replaced by the Security State Bank.

The **Gilroy** family could not make it to the parade due to the death of **Mrs. James Gilroy**.

The most exciting news in town is the organization of the Cannon Valley Telephone Company with **J.J. Worlein** as its president. About 25 new telephones were already installed.

Attorney **Dullam** was walking the parade route passing out leaflets to arouse interest in favor of a lecture course. It had been rumored that one of his first lectures was to be about the over population of the bullhead and what can be done about it.

Any idea who is leading the band?

The other furniture factory

Waterville had two furniture factories at one time. This photo was taken in the early 1900's and shows the interior of the factory that was located in the area of the Waterville Creamery, south of town. **Mr. Aberley** (the father of **Betty Aberley Schwartz**) is shown standing in the middle. Do you know the names of the other two men?

Trees for furniture, lakes for fishing, tourists, and ice, wheat and corn for flour and feed—Waterville prospered by its abundance of natural resources. Thanks to people like **Mr. Aberley**, Waterville was recognized as a community that had much to offer its citizens. And, it still does today.

James Simpson passed away. Pallbearers were Wyatt Deming, Leo Stangler, John Schmidt, Ed Goltz, Don Werner, and Lowell Rieke. (1961)

Greetings from Waterville, Minn.

Views of Waterville Residences, or "Who lives in that house?"

Birdseye View of Waterville, Minn. looking North.

(Many of the homes featured in this section are standing somewhere in and around Waterville. The location for some has been determined. There is some uncertainty about others. Your mission, should you decide to accept it, is to determine their exact location.)

A bird's-eye view of Waterville

This card was published for **Dr. Clay's** Pharmacy in 1909. Can you find: (1) a train, (2) the Catholic Church, (3) Nicollet Hotel (**George Greer's** garage), (4) the old furniture factory, (5) the old post office, and (6) Lake Sakatah? You're right, you will need a magnifying glass. This picture was taken from the hill behind the Catholic Church.

"Tell the fair haired Swede that I'll be back soon" wrote **Ed** to **Mr. Henry Hanson** in Albert Lea.

J.S. Lawless has 25 houses for sale in Waterville. (1914)

Greetings from Waterville, Minn.

Waterville North Side

The North Side Sewing Club will meet with **Mrs. Pauline Haase** on Tuesday." That was the *Advance* news of February 24, 1943. The North Side Club has enough history to write their own book. Of all of my postcards of Waterville, this is one of my favorites.

On September 13, 1932 the North Side Club held their first meeting at the home of **Mrs. Etta Atherton** with 14 members present. During the span of 40 years 80 ladies have been members of the club. Charter members of the club were **Etta Atherton, Mabel Grobe, Bernice Moench** and **Ida Mae Perkins.**

This photo will date in the 1910-1920 era. Can you imagine what this road looked like in the spring?

I don't know who the children are but they are talking about the horse trader who came to town last Tuesday. It's not unusual to have a horse trader come through but he happened to have a horse with five feet. A large crowd of spectators saw the freak (i.e. the horse).

"The making of friends"

The purpose of the North Side Club was to have a friendly get together every two weeks on Tuesday afternoon. They always remembered all the newlyweds, gave a token of welcome to new babies, a card of cheer when needed and fruit and flowers to the ill.

When the club was five years old, **Ida Burgess** wrote a poem that tells why the North Side Club will always be an important part of Waterville's history.

> *Life is sweet just because of friends we've made,*
> *And the things in common we have.*
> *We want to live on, not because of ourselves,*
> *but because of the people who care.*
> *It's giving and doing for somebody else,*
> *on that all life's splendor depends.*
> *And the joy of this world when it's all added up,*
> *Is found in the Making of Friends.*

The person that sent this 1900 card may have been staying at the Waterville hospital under **Dr. Cory's** care. The patient was suspected of possibly having lockjaw.

Walker's Pool Hall was moved from the Kapoun building to the Quirk building on Third Street. (1914)

Greetings from Waterville, Minn.

Farmstead: What's mom cooking?

Mail was delivered on the north side of Lake Tetonka in the vehicle on the right. In the winter the little house on wheels was placed on a sled. **Bert Ryan**, the photographer of many of these postcards was the rural mail carrier.

This place is believed to be north of town a few miles on the County Road 11 to Highway 13. **Grace Rosenberg** lived there with her father. Maybe you have a better idea as to where this farmstead is.

This card goes back to the early 1900's. This means grandpa in the photo was born well before the Civil War and probably fought in the Civil War. The smoke is coming from the chimney, there's a bunch of vines located on the front porch (Do you know why?) and Mom is cooking up her favorite stew. The people took time off from their chores to pose for photographer **Ryan** who was there to deliver mail. Dad was happy to receive his latest *Farm Journal* featuring an article "You, too, can spend a few weeks in Florida—Here's how."

Life was hard with or without Florida.

The John Weaver Home

I will always remember this as the **John Weaver** home even though he merely rented an apartment in this stately Victorian home. **John** served as police chief for many years when the police force consisted of **John** and (well, I guess he was it).

This house is still standing south of the post office. **Bob Mills** built this home and, as a local contractor, he built many other homes in the first quarter of the 20th century.

One of the men in front is **Mr. Mills**. He is probably talking about the eleven varieties of coal available at **Fahning** and Lampert Lumber Company. A home this size took a lot of coal.

A boy was born to Mr. and Mrs. Ray Volkman. (1956)

Greetings from Waterville, Minn.

Louis Dusbabek Cottage

This is a 1918 photo of a Lake Tetonka cottage. These Lake Tetonka cottages were the forerunners of things to come -- namely, resorts.

This is the **Louis Dusbabek** Cottage. It is still standing on the east side of Lake Tetonka. Across the street was the Silver Streak skating rink and dance hall. At one time the cabin belonged to **Bill Farrington** who was also the editor of the *Waterville Advance*.

The land was granted to **Lewis Snell** in 1857. **Louis Dusbabek** and his wife, **Amelia,** purchased the land from **George Snow** in October, 1916. The cabin was purchased by **W.S. Farrington** on August 16, 1929. The home was in the **Farrington** family until August of 1962 when it was purchased by **Robert Townsend** of Altoona, Iowa. The house remains pretty much the same as it was then. Imagine the sun setting on silhouetted fishing boats on Lake Tetonka. Over the years thousands of scenes similar to this were observed by cottage owners sitting on their docks and porches. Just sitting—that's nice.

Farm Home and Wedding Plans

Wouldn't you just love to go inside this home and take a look? I wonder what they had for lunch. This photo was taken around Waterville but I don't know where. Do you? **Mrs. Bert Ryan** is the woman standing on the far left.

It looks like the two men are brothers. The wife is pregnant. Photographer **Ryan** had to do a little coaxing to get the people to pose for a photo in the middle of the day. "OK, but we get a free photo." So they gathered up a couple of dining room chairs and set them on the front lawn in the light.

The couple asked **Bert** if he had been asked to take the photos at the forthcoming marriage of **Gertrude Roemhildt** to **Leo Hopkins**, sheriff of Le Sueur County. He said he never discussed his clients but he did say the wedding would be held at the Trinity Lutheran Church and the public was invited (June 27, 1948).

A house warming was given for Mr. and Mrs. Arthur Bartelt. Snouse was played. Mrs. Leslie Comstock won the lady's prize. (1944)

Page 10-4

Greetings from Waterville, Minn.

Seidle's Cottage Lake Tetonka

𝒶 note in the 1914 *Sentinel* read, "**J.E. Seidle's** cottage on Lake Tetonka Boulevard is now completed. It is the finest cottage on our lakes." The cottage was located west of **Renshaw's** resort. **Bob Dusbabek** built his home where this cottage once stood. In later years it belonged to **Mr. Bill Warburton**.

Can't you just picture yourself sitting in this screened in porch on a quiet July evening, visiting with friends and watching the mallards swim by your dock?

J.E. Seidle operated a drug store in Waterville. He was as surprised as most were when he heard that the Commercial Hotel was to be sold on July 17 (1914) to **O.B. Emerson. P. J. Gutzler** was the previous owner.

That's **Mr.** and **Mrs. Seidle** sitting in the front. Hotels didn't concern them at the time. They have a new cottage to call home.

Waterville's Christian Hill?

𝐼f you brought guests to Waterville from the south, you probably drove down South 3rd Street. I have heard some people call this "Christian Hill" but I can't verify it. Others referred to it as "Silk Stocking Hill." Large homes were shaded by giant elms and it gave visitors to Waterville a stately, clean looking, clean living, first impression. It was home to the **Eblings, Balfe's, Sheehy's, Dr. Holten's, Jim Lawless** and **Pat** and **Jane Drews.**

It's 1961 and people are talking about the recent fire that destroyed the home of **Guy Kelley**. There was also a fire at H & S Logging. **Nancy Zachman** was recently selected Homemaker of Tomorrow. **John Nelson** will move from his present location to the former Gem Theatre building. **Dave Rosenau** scored 17 points in a victory over Waseca Sacred Heart. **Walter Bittrich** has been confined to his home for several weeks due to a serious illness. **Herman Solyntjes** is taking a course in electronics at Faribault High School. **Neil Wetzel** clinched a Waterville wrestling decision over Ellendale with a 7-3 win.

Christ Gish has three nice lots for sale in West Waterville at low prices. (1955)

Page 10-5

Greetings from Waterville, Minn.

The big white house

Doc Brady's Dance Pavilion is the building you see to the left of the big white house. **Bruce** and **Ruth Cummins** are the proud owners of this house located on the east side of Lake Tetonka. The now well traveled road in front of the home is just a dirt path in this 1930's photo.

Imagine people sitting on the front porch in their rockers and listening to the sounds of fun and laughter from **Doc's** Place. The Lager's Novelty Radio Orchestra has returned by popular demand. The gents' admission was 40 cents and the ladies were charged 10 cents. **Hiller Teff** (rural mail carrier) and his orchestra would also frequently play at **Doc's**.

News in 1933 that the Pavilion goers may have talked about included: **August Messall** and family attended a surprise party at the **Frank Schultz** home. The **Ed Lamont** family visited the home of **Fred Lamont**. **Mrs. Frank Luker** is taking treatments at St. Lucas hospital and doing nicely. **Jane Stowe** celebrated her eleventh birthday.

Northside home—Which one?

Bill Haase was the former owner of this home located on the east side of 1st Street. It is still standing.

Bill may be the one in the photo who is asking his wife if she had heard the latest news about Hitler. "Yeh." he says, "People are saying Hitler is a vegetarian. He acts like a man who lives on poison ivy."

Bill recently advertised a brooder house stove for sale in the *Advance* want ads. The *Advance* reports that "the stove was sold promptly and **Mr. Haase** informed us that he could have sold two or three more."

Marzahn's Tips (a popular feature in the Waterville *Advance*) reports that **Henry Pommeranz's** horses are happy because he has purchased a McCormick-Deering mower.

Willard Goltz is completing his residence on his farm just west of town. (1947)

Greetings from Waterville, Minn.

Country Victorian home

Do you recogize this place? It could be in Waterville or in the immediate area. If you know, let me know.

The two women in the picture are waiting to go into town to do some shopping at **Suchomel's** store. **Mr. Suchomel** just rented the **Bill Haase** building and he is selling out his stock in the building he is presently renting. He has men's shirts for 24 cents and men't silk ties for 49 cents. Corn Flakes are nine cents per package.

They also plan to take in the show at the Gem where Shirley Temple is starring in *Rebecca of Sunny Brook Farm*. The year is 1938.

Mort and who?

Mort **Mengis** made the rounds in his early days. I don't know who the other people are and I don't know where the house is located in Waterville. Maybe you do.

The young boy sitting on the steps was expecting **Mort** to deliver a Captain Midnight Decoder Ring but he had no such luck.

A lot of people are thankful for their homes. The fire department in 1931 responded to a call at the **Isaac Peach** farm, but too late to save the nice farm home.

Al Robson is home after spending some time at the Owatonna Nursing home in 1961. Al is the former president of Citizen's State Bank. People are reminded that Al likes visitors.

Mr. Underwood, operator of the Waterville Creamery, believes the first annual creamery picnic was a big success. (1938)

Greetings from Waterville, Minn.

Herman's Home

Herman Schulz, grandfather of **Paul Schulz**, knew how to live. Not only did he own one of Waterville's best hotels (the Commercial Hotel), he also owned one of Waterville's finer homes. This home is located in the 300 block of West Main Street.

That's **Herman**, a native of Germany, sitting on the porch. He's thinking he should be working in the hotel because he's trying out a new clerk. Plus, people have been saying that bank robbers are using the hotel as a hideout. "Just plain foolishness," **Herman** says.

Louise is also sitting on the porch next to **Bertha Pischel** who is caring for the baby. **Bertha** worked for the **Schulz's**. **Louise** is just happy to be enjoying this nice summer day. They went to church in the morning and she has hinted to **Herman** to make some home made ice cream for this evening. **Louise** also knew how to live.

Good taste in Waterville home

My father liked to take pictures and he said it was about time he took a picture of our new home (about 1947). That's my mother sitting in front. The white frame home was located between Herbert and Mill Street on Hoosac Street. If you were to ask me an hour ago what street I lived on, I could not have told you.

The house had a cement front porch as you see. My brother and I used our artistic talent one day to draw on it with crayolas and my mother used her parenting talent to have us scrub it off. My dad had a beautiful garden on the east side. He was proud of his roses and gladiolas. It was a good size lot that my dad mowed with a push lawn mower.

The house has many great memories for me. Christmas, Easter, birthday parties—I think I was the only boy in town who invited just girls to his birthday party. Pictured in the photo on the right are (back row) **Joyce Miller, Jeanette Koelzer, Sandra Hamele, Gretchen Rausch,** (front row) **Mary Roemhildt, Vicky Meyers, Sharon Chambers,** and **Jennifer Rausch**. I had good taste.

Ben Wiese has a five room house for rent. Phone 330. (1957)

"I came to Waterville in 1901. I was nine years old." *Jack Sikel*

(a bird's eye view of Waterville's early history)

Emerging from the timber belt, we reach Waterville, a gem of a town, beautifully located between two lakes, upon one of which, during the season of navigation, a little steamer awaits you, running down to Morristown. Evidence of prosperity are here visible on every hand. The place is full of business, and the citizens happy and contented, as they have every reason to be. (a Minneapolis paper, 1887)

"...and the citizens happy and contented, as they have every reason to be."

When people are happy and content, you can't hope for much more. No doubt, this was the primary reason for Waterville's early pioneers to settle here. Of course there were the lakes, some decent farm land and plenty of game. And, you would have to think that Waterville would become a prosperous community—it had a lot going for it. Many people are still waiting for the "prosperous" community but most would admit that Watervillians should feel pleased.

The name of Waterville was suggested by **E.L. Wright,** a native of Waterville, Maine. He surveyed the town of Waterville in 1856. Some of the early pioneers were **David Parsons, N. Paquone, James Shonts, Mitty Shonts, N. Paquone, D.J. Hitchcock,** and **Eliza Farquire.** Other enterprising pioneers were **Jacob Dawald, Samuel Drake, Michael Ferch, Lewis Stowe, Amos Robinson,** and **Charles Christman.**

Mr. Tidball was the first pioneer to build a frame building and open a general store at the present day site of Waterville. A **Mr. Rogers** followed **Mr. Tidball** by building another general store around the same time and stocking it with merchandise that he brought with him. At approximately the same time

S.Sgt. Benjamin Kniefel is home on furlough from Camp Rucker, Ala. (1952)

Greetings From Waterville, Minn.

Mr. Drake built a hotel and shortly afterwards was made the first postmaster. The first transaction of any mail was a large one as it was all carried in a cigar box. A hotel was also built by a **Mr. Jacob Dawald** and Waterville was starting to take shape.

In 1870 **John Broadbent** started a brick yard. He furnished the brick for the first brick building erected in Waterville at the corner of Common and Sixth Street by **William Cummons.**

Jacob Dawald established the oldest hotel in Waterville in 1857. It was named the Waterville House and had a convenient barn connected. It was located on the corner where the Gem Theatre stood. The Minnesota House was started in 1877 by **Herman G. Schulz.** It accommodated sixteen guests.

In September of 1876, Waterville had an unexpected visitor, Jesse James. Jesse James stopped at the Waterville House Hotel, before he went on to Northfield where he attempted to rob the bank on September 7, 1876. Records indicate Waterville seemed to have been a favorite place for horse thieves to congregate and that horses were recovered here quite often.

One of the major businesses in the 1880's was the ginseng market started by the **Tilden** brothers. It grew in abundance in the "Big Woods." Ginseng provided a source of income for early settlers and sold for six to twenty-five cents per pound. The ginseng season began in September.

> "Tetonka Flour" was known nationally.

The first person to die in Waterville was a young son of **Mr. and Mrs. Drake** who died of small pox in 1855. The following spring another son was born in the **Drake** home. This was the first birth. The first wedding was that of **Michael Ferch** and **Francisca Densbabach** in 1856. The first school was taught by **Miss Davidson** in 1857 with 13 children in attendance.

> The Episcopal Church is the oldest building in Waterville..

In 1866 a furniture factory was started. The lathe in this factory was turned by horse power and the horse was ridden **by Wick Beach** for the salary of ten cents a day.

Waterville is rich in Indian history—some of it infamous. The last Sioux battle and last Indian scalping took place in Waterville. **Son Luker** (1881-1977) used to hunt in what now is Sakatah State Park. At the age of nine he recalls seeing the old foundation of what used to be the Faribault Fur Trading Post.

Both "Sakatah" and "Tetonka" are Sioux names. Sioux Indians lived on the shores of our lakes. They hunted and fished and raised their families. No doubt, they also were friends with Waterville's early pioneers. As was said earlier, Waterville had the dubious honor of taking the last Sioux scalp to end the Sioux Uprising of 1862. Waterville was the only town in the area that felt safe during the scare. In the end, President Lincoln would give the order to hang 38 Sioux at Mankato. The Sioux that were left were exiled from Minnesota..

In 1882 the Cannon Valley Railroad was built from Red Wing to Waterville. After the coming of the Minneapolis and St. Louis Railroad in 1877 Waterville had quite an economic boom. The village was incorporated in 1878 and the following officers elected: **L. Z. Rogers**, President of the council; **H. J. Carlton** and **D. El. Potter** Councilmen; **Martin Segar**, Marshal; **A.N. Roberts**, Assessor and **William Green**, Justice of the Peace.

Waterville had a lime kiln in the late 70's under the ownership of **Dave Temple**. He gathered lime along the lake shore.

The Episcopalians were the first to hold religious services in the town in 1858. The Episcopal Church is the oldest building in Waterville. It was begun

Greetings From Waterville, Minn.

in 1870 and completed in 1874.

In 1873, **Dr. E. P. Case** came here to practice medicine. He erected a hospital on the north side of Lower Sakatah. It was later destroyed by fire. There was also a traveling doctor, **Dr. Davis**, who gathered herbs as he traveled about, and brewed his own medicine. People felt that he was very successful in his practice.

> **The farming country surrounding us is of the best. All farmers in our locality are becoming wealthy.**

"Tetonka Flour" was known nationally and was the brain child of **Merrick** and **Melhorn**. The flour mill was built on the east side in the 70's and was purchased in 1883 by **James Quirk**.

In the 1890's there was a large furniture factory; a flour mill, a woolen mill, a sash and door mill, a hospital, a photographic studio, a feed mill, a cigar factory, a machine shop, a wagon shop, a furniture store, a drug store, and a fish market. There were two banks, two millinery shops, two restaurants, two dry goods stores, two tailor shops, two meat markets, two barber shops, two lumber yards (Lampert Yards on Hoosac Street and **August Heckert** built a lumber yard on Main Street).

Waterville continued to grow in the early 1900's. There were three hardware stores, 3 livery barns, 3 lawyers, 4 doctors, 4 hotels, 4 blacksmiths, 6 general stores, 7 saloons, a creamery, a chair factory, two Chinese laundries, 2 cigar factories, 4 barber shops and 6 churches. Butter was 12 cents a pound and cord wood was $3 a cord.

This growth is just what Waterville's business community, no doubt, prayed for and received. A description of Waterville sent out by the Waterville Commercial Club in 1913 said this about Waterville: *"Waterville, LeSueur County, is one of the best small towns to be found in Minnesota. Our business men are all of the up-to-date courteous kind. Our schools are rated second to none in Minnesota. We have in our midst the following factories: a fine pickle factory; a large furniture factory which ships its output all over the United States; planing mill; one of the greatest plants for the making of Amber Cane Syrup which is pure; one fine machine shop; and grain elevator. Our schools are rated second to none in Minnesota. We have eight churches and fourteen lodges. The present population of Waterville is about 1,400 and we are rapidly increasing. The farming country surrounding us is of the best. All farmers in our locality are becoming wealthy."*

> **At one time over 25 families made a living by fishing.**

The population of Waterville in various years was: 1873: 400, 1890: 937, 1900: 1200, 1920: 1289, 1940: 1382, 1960: 1475, 1970: 1600.

In the early 1900's, acreage sold from $80 - $120, in 1960 it was around $200-$400 per acre.

In 1908 Waterville saw 3 new buildings under construction: Security State Bank, school, and the telephone office.

Fishing was always a part of Waterville's history. At one time over 25 families made a living by fishing.

In 1911 electricity came to Waterville. The first auto came to town in 1909. **Charlie Christman** was the salesman. **Ira Huffington, Fred Zollner,** and **Mr. Hartwick** each purchased an auto for $600.00.

Other establishments that existed in Waterville during its early years in the 1900's were the following:

Banks: Security State Bank (1908) and First National Bank (1904)
General Merchandise: **George E. Greene, Ruedy Bros., Riley** and **Marzahn**

Sylvia Roemhildt won one dollar for bowling a game of 165 in 1940.

Grocers: **H.H. Stowe, C.H. Bliss, Ruedy Bros., Riley** and **Marzahn**
Dry Goods: **George Greene** and **Riley** and **Marzahn**
Furniture: **J.J. Worlein** and Co.
Harness and Saddlery, Robes, Blankets and Whips: **H. J. Fritz**
Sorghum Manufacturer: **Leslie Fowler**
Photographer: **C.W. Christman**
Ladies and Gents Furnishings: **George Greene**
Drugs, Books and Stationery: **J.E. Seidle**
Flour and Feed: **C.A. Backman**
Notions: **Ruedy** Bros.
Real Estate Loans: Security State Bank and First National Bank
Bakery: The Star (**D. Corcoran**, Prop.) and **Joseph Miller**
Furniture Factory: Waterville Furniture Co.
Ford Automobile Supplies: **C.W. Christman**
Crockery and China Ware: **Ruedy Bros., C.H. Bliss, H.H. Stowe, Riley** and **Marzahn**
Steam and Hot Water Heating: **Callies** and **Zellmer**
Lumber: Central Lumber Co.
Shoes: **H.H. Stowe, George Greene, Riley** and **Marzahn**
Poultry and Eggs, Hides and Furs: **C.A. Backman**
Undertakers, Carpets and Rugs: **J.J. Worlein** and Co.
Sheet Metal Works and Job Work: **Callies** and **Zellmer**
Confectionery and Fruits: The Star Restaurant and Bakery, **Joseph Miller**
Insurance, Real Estate: Security State Bank, First National Bank, **J.S. Lawless**
Manufacturer of Rye, buckwheat and Graham Flour, Custom Feed Grinding: **Fred Zollner**
Pianos, Organs, and Monuments: **J.J. Worlein** and Co.
Millinery: **George E. Greene**
Wall Paper: **J.E.Seidle, J.J. Worlein**
Shoe and Harness Repairing: **H.J. Fritz**
Tubular Well Drilling and Repairing: **Leslie Fowler**
Restaurant: The Star Restaurant and Bakery and **Joseph Miller**
Coal, Paints and Oils: Central Lumber & Co.
Bakery Heating Plants: **Joseph Miller**
Livery, Feed and Sale Barn: **H.D. Cram**
Hardware: **F.A. Lowe, G.T. Murray, Hancuh, Dusbabek**
Cement, Brick, and Building Material: Central Lumber Co.
Commercial Book and Job Printing: *The Waterville Sentinel*

Waterville Auto Company has Chevrolets for sale at $595. (1927)

Newspaper: *The Waterville Sentinel*
Pickle Factory: the J.S. Gedney Pickle Co.
Stock Farm: **P. O'Leary, C.W. Glotfelter**
Plumbers and Tinners: **Callies** and **Zellmer**
General Blacksmithing and Horse Shoeing: **Jargo** and Son

Some of the comments by **Jack Sikel** were used in this brief early history of Waterville. I don't claim to be a historian but I know that first hand experience is the best teacher. **Jack** has much to teach us about Waterville and I am happy to see our oldest citizen's recollections occasionally printed in the *Lake Region Life*.

Jack Sikel, Mason Marzahn, Uzada Salmon, Hazel Allen, Mabel Walz, Mary Lou and **Herman Solyntjes, my parents, Bernadine Hildebrant** are a few of a declining number of Watervillians who are its true historians. Some day you will be among them and some day someone will come and ask you, "Do you know anything about . . . ?" I hope this book will help you find the answer.

AL & RAY MOTORS
Al Volkman and Ray Knish

- DANCE -
Benefit Veterans of Foreign Wars
Sponsored by Auxiliary
At Brady's Pavilion--Waterville
Monday, Sept. 10th
Music by Teff's Orchestra
EVERYBODY INVITED!
Tickets—including tax—60c

JACOBSON'S
STORE AND WAREHOUSES
WATERVILLE, MINN
PHONE ORDERS CALL 24

Art's Repair Shop
Art Roeglin, Prop.

Roemhildt's Restaurant
Short Orders
Lunches
Soft Drinks
Ice Cream
Cigars
Tobacco
Cigarettes

IT IS TIME NOW
TO START FEEDING
---EGG MASH---
WE SELL OURS
AT A PRICE YOU CAN
AFFORD TO PAY
TRY A SACK AND WATCH
.....RESULTS....
ZOLLNER'S MILL
PHONE 7   WE DELIVER

When you have some free time, take a walk around Sakatah Cemetery. Many of the names mentioned in this brief early history of Waterville can be found there on tombstones. When you walk among its gray and white granite markers, its shady solitude and greenery, listen as closely as you are looking The spirits of our early pioneers have a message for you.

What's the message? If I told you, you wouldn't believe me. Plus, my words would never do justice to what they are saying to you. You will have to go and discover it for yourself. The only thing I can say is that when you do hear it, your life will never be the same again.

Miss Myra Wetzel was awarded an electric toaster for a question she submitted on the Gluek program on WCCO radio. (1951)

Greetings From Waterville, Minn.

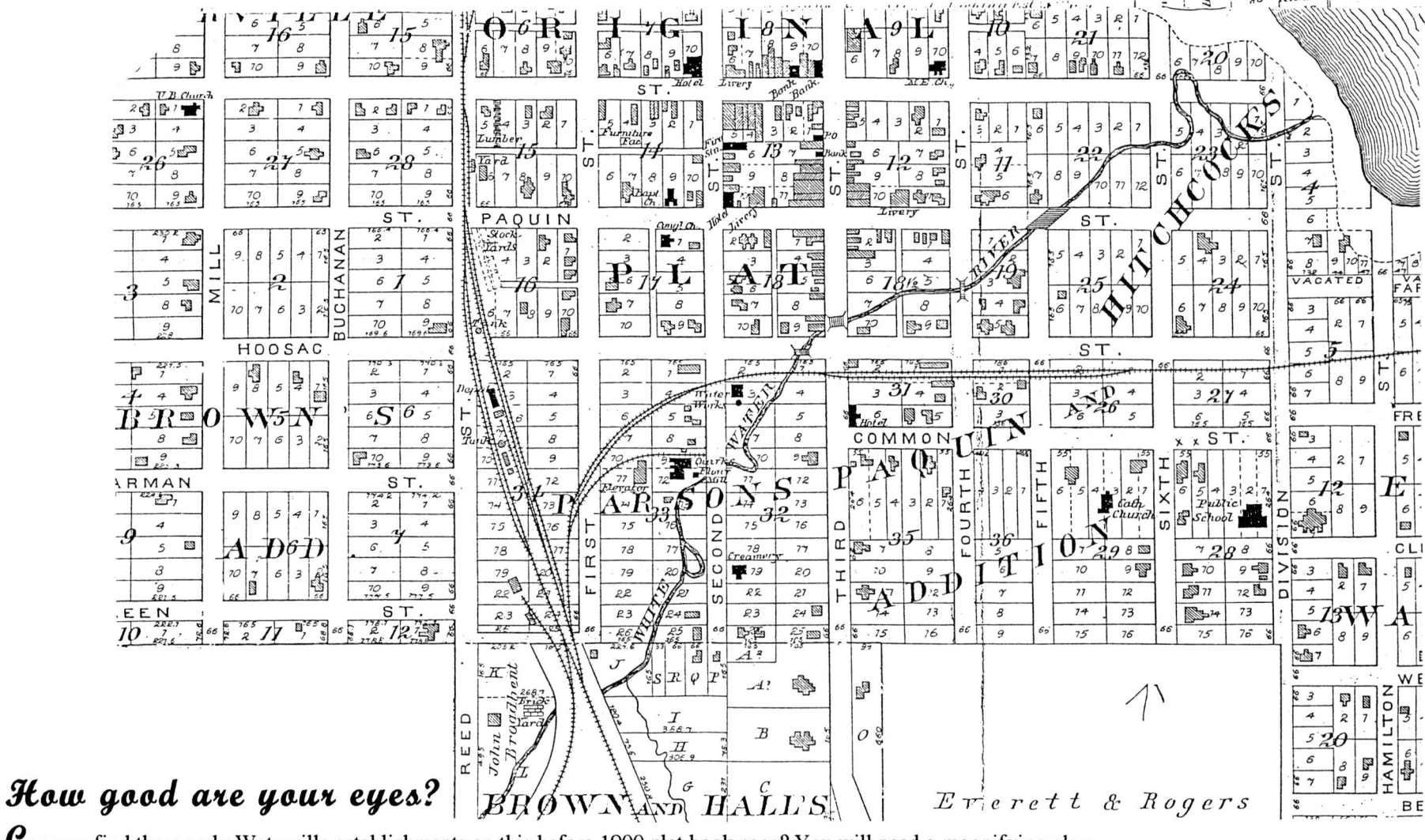

How good are your eyes?

Can you find these early Waterville establishments on this before 1900 plat book page? You will need a magnifying glass.

___water works	___three hotels	___three banks	___Methodist Church	___Congregational Church
___Baptist Church	___Catholic Church	___school	___creamery	___flour mill
___fire station	___U.B. Church	___depot	___stock yards	___brick yard
___furniture factory	___livery	___elevator	___post office	

Did you notice the bank building and post office in the vicinity of **Dusbabek's** Market? How about the bank building on the corner where the post office was located? There is a hotel south of **Fahnings**. Is it the Minnesota or the Waterville Hotel?

Mary Comstock has accepted a position as medical secretary at St. Joseph Hospital in Mankato. (1957)

Page 11-6

Greetings From Waterville, Minn.

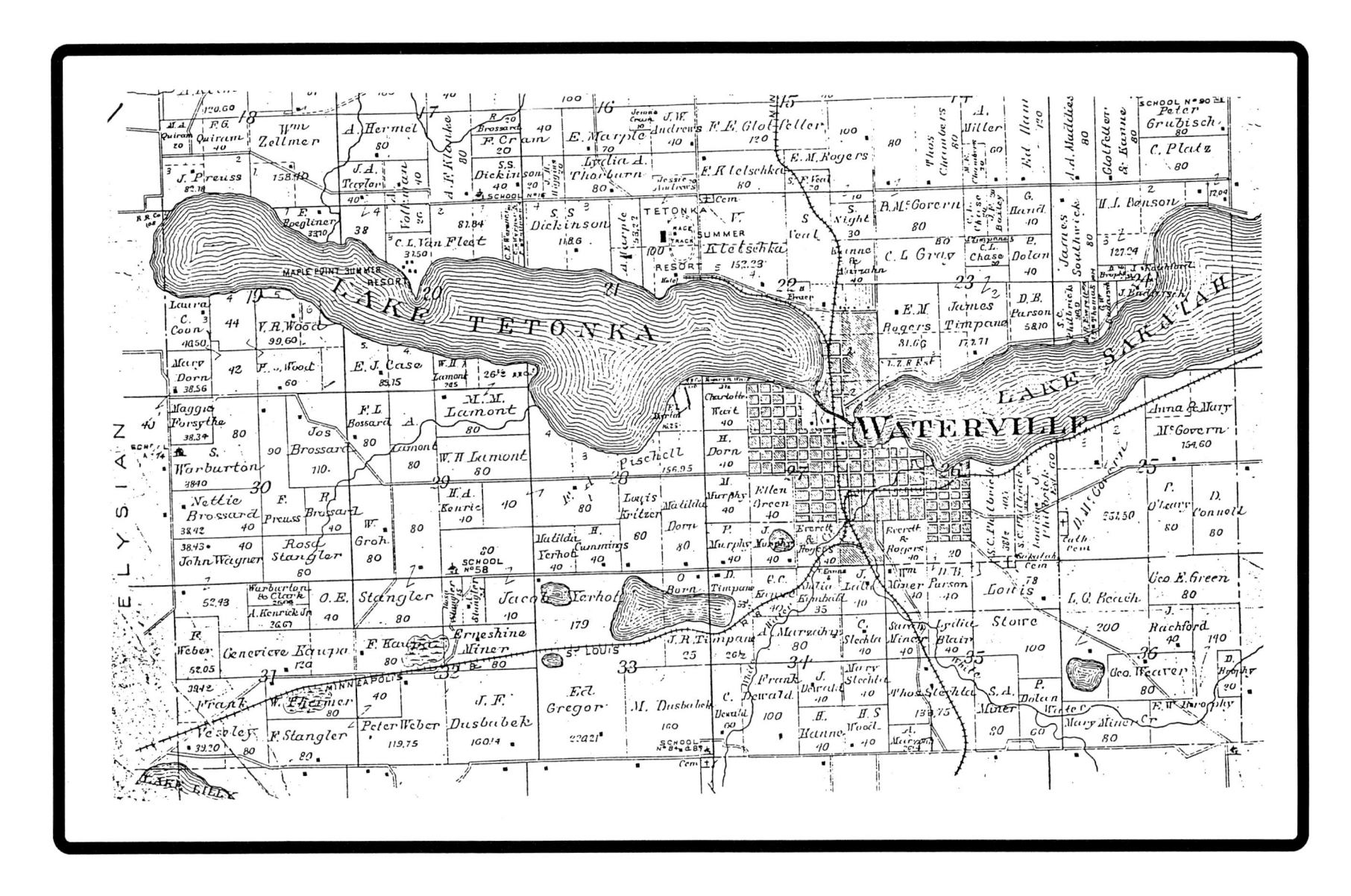

How many are your relatives?

You will see some familiar last names on this early plat book page of Waterville. They are the people who saw a town between two lakes and began the task of building it. They left a fine legacy for us. How many are related to you? **Stowe, Beach, O'Leary, Miner, Slechta, Dawald, Dusbabek, Gregor, Lamont, Dickinson, Gray, Rogers, Timpane, Murphy, Dorn, Everett, Weaver, McGovern, Kletschka, Glotfelter, Hermel, Zellmer, Groh, Stangler, Grubish, Marzahn.**

Fred Brandt has aluminum doors for $43.00 at Central Lumber. (1960)

I remember...

A primary reason for writing this book was to document some of the history of Waterville using old postcards to help people reflect on what Waterville was.

Another reason for the book was intended for those who come after us so they will know something about Waterville when they begin to wonder and ask, "I wonder what Waterville was like when . . ."

A third reason for writing this book is personal. Writers write for themselves; they write what first pleases them and they hope that what they write will also please others. This book gives me the opportunity to reflect on the Waterville that I knew during the first quarter century of my life. What follows are some of the things I remember. I hope that my personal recollection will also cause you to remember some special times about Waterville.

Sledding on Kritzer's Hill

*I*magine a cold winter night when the streets are icy and snow packed and the only light is from the street lights. Imagine, also, a half dozen or so young boys, walking up a hill pulling wooden sleds with steel runners. They don't say much as their breath turns into clouds of white mist. They are saving their energy for the fun that is to come. Occasionally a few fall on the icy street.

For my brother **Craig, Roland** and **Dennis Bittrich, Clarence Harriman, David Rosenau** and at times other neighbors, sledding on **Marlin Kritzer's** Hill (the very west end of Main Street) was our Winter Olympics. The challenge of **Kritzer's** Hill was threefold. First, you took a long run holding on to the sides of your sled and then slamming it down with your body on top of it. The faster you ran and the more you were able to throw your body forward, the farther you would be able to slide. If you got a good run you could easily make the right turn on to Herbert Street. That was the second challenge. If you got a very good run and the street was especially icy you could make the turn down Mill Street past the old United Brethren Church (now **Wayne Prosch's** Funeral Home). The third challenge was staying on your sled while other sledders tried to pull and push you off while sliding down **Kritzer's** Hill.

State officials urge schools to postpone the opening of school until September 16 due to the state polio epidemic. (1946)

Page 12-1

High School snake dances and bonfires:

The Thursday night before the Friday homecoming game was Waterville's Super Bowl celebration. It began with the coronation in the gym in front of a standing room only crowd followed by the bonfire.

The homecoming bonfires were a spectacular sight. For weeks seniors would round up anything made of wood and rubber to burn. The pile of scrap lumber would be two or three stories high topped off by an outhouse or two. Flames shot up like sky rockets and it was impossible to get within 50 feet of the fire. The Waterville Fire Department was parked out of sight just in case those crazy kids did something crazy. But they understood because many of the firemen had been one of those crazy kids themselves.

After a few cheers from the cheerleaders, the evening was topped off by the snake dance — Waterville's version of Valley Fair. Led by the cheerleaders, kids of all ages would hold hands making a line of 150 to 300 kids — older ones at the head of the line, younger ones towards the end. You hung on for your life as the snake of wild-eyed, daring, dashing kids ran through the streets of Waterville around the cast iron street light poles and in between the parked '57 Chevrolets and '55 Fords.

I'm not sure where or how the dance ended but I do know that this emotional event never really ended in the hearts of the Waterville kids.

I remember that Coach **Dahl** would remind the football players not to participate in the snake dance because of fear of injury. But that was like telling an Iowa tourist not to fish bullheads.

As I think about why kids in those days didn't get too excited about the artificial highs of alcohol and drugs, we got our highs from the bonfires and snake dances — naturally.

Backman's chickens

If you caught them alive after they escaped from the hatchery, **Charley Backman** would give you five cents. If you brought them back dead, I don't think you received anything.

This was a marvelous pastime on our way home from school. We would go inside to ask for the chicken catchers (a piece of thick wire with a hook on the end for going around the chicken's leg), the perfect tool for those chickens that tried to hide under cars.

Since **Backman's** would also sell baby chickens to farmers to raise, they would occasionally throw some eggs away that didn't hatch or that weren't exactly perfect. We would go behind the hatchery and check the steel barrels to rescue any discarded eggs that were about to hatch. One year we took home three or four chicks to raise. They turned out to be the meanest chickens east of Elysian. I can understand why **Backman's** threw them away.

Bob Dellwo

If there were ever a fan of Waterville High School athletics, it was **Bob Dellwo**. He knew the athletes and his familiar and friendly face was always a welcome sight for me. He was a frequent baseball umpire for all levels of baseball. **Bob** always seemed to be there — win or lose. Thanks, **Bob**.

Gerald Preuss is best man at the Ruth Watzek, Art Sorgatz wedding. (1952)

"Watch out for snapping turtles!"

On the east side of "Waterville's Old Swimming Hole" (i.e. Waterville's swimming beach) in Lake Tetonka was a swamp. We spent more time on the logs and rocks in the swamp than we did swimming. We caught tadpoles and imagined all kinds of big and ugly water creatures that lurked in the swamp waters.

Each summer swimming lessons would be offered and I eventually learned how to swim. The test of your swimming ability came when you were able to swim out to the raft where the "big kids" hung out. Still, the excitement of going to the beach was not the beach or the raft, but the imaginary creatures we all knew hid in the swamp.

When the swamp was filled in the creatures moved into Lake Tetonka where they hang out in the deepest waters.

The old timers tell of Waterville's Sturgeon that is as long as a 16 foot boat. Only a few people have actually seen Waterville's sea monster. But it's there—just waiting to emerge to keep the story alive.

Dudley's Red Owl:

I owe my work ethics to my parents and to **John Dudley**. The thing I learned most from **John** was to find something to do when there was nothing to do—which didn't happen too often.

John always kept us on our toes so when he left to go to lunch or go home for the evening, we could relax a bit. I may have relaxed a little too much the time I threw a two pound bag of powdered sugar to **Don O'Brien** from one end of the store to the other. The bag bounced off of the ceiling, broke open and showered **Don** and all of the shelving around it with fine, white, powdered sugar. Remnants may still be there.

I worked for **John** for 10 years as I was going through school--as much as 57 hours per week. He started his boys out at 65 cents an hour--the going rate. When I left I was making a $1.25. **Bill Rieke, Gary Salmon**, my brother, **Craig, Harold Schwichtenberg, Darwin Wild, Curtis Stangler, Don O'Brien, Herb Beach, Helen Eggers, Celia Stoering, Mel Schultz, Roger Schwartz, Dennis Morris** were some of the many people that worked for **John** while I worked there.

Clerking, carrying out groceries, stocking shelves, working in the produce section—I enjoyed the variety. What I didn't enjoy was carrying in the 100 pound sacks of potatoes. Every once in awhile you would get a bag with a few rotten ones in it. The smell of a rotten potato is something you don't easily forget.

Business was booming on Saturday evenings—the best times at the store. Area farmers came to town to do their weekly shopping. It was not unusual for someone to spend a $20 bill for a week's supply of groceries. Can you imagine?

I had worked there so many years that I could recite the price of every item and knew the shopping habits of the customers. For example, **Mr. Townsend**, who lived north of Lake Sakatah, would buy 10-12 cans of sweet potatoes and a half dozen two pound loaves of Red Owl bread that sold for twenty cents a loaf.

We would close up at 9:00 and spend another hour cleaning the store and preparing it for Monday. On Sunday the store rested. It was a great time and I have **John** and **Kathleen Dudley** to thank.

Lard and sugar and fresh bread

To this day I can taste the fresh, home rendered lard sprinkled with sugar and spread on freshly baked bread. It was a treat that only **Dorothy Bittrich** provided.

In my early days, our home away from home was the **Walt Bittrich** place. With **Joe** and **Dennis, Hank, Henry, Bob, Irene, Bernice,** and **Esther**, there was always something going on there and always something to eat.

Glenn's Bakery

Glenn Preuss started a tradition of baking the best bread, bismarks and fried cinnamon rolls south of the Twin Cities.

Glenn's Bakery was more than a bakery—it was on my list of places to stop while going home from school. **Alma Raedeke**, my grandmother, worked there as did **Agnes Raedeke**, my aunt, and **Ruth Rosenau**, mother to my good friend, **David**. The fresh bakery smells and friendly greetings combined to make a winning recipe for me.

Molly worked up front and **Glenn** would be in back cleaning up and preparing for the next day. If he wasn't there he would probably be out on the lake or in the duck blind.

Glenn sold the bakery to **Garland Livingood**. He has kept the tradition. It's still the best bakery in southern Minnesota.

See the 1949 Ford at Barrett Motor Co. in Waterville. "The Ford in your future." (1948)

Lutheran Church Ladies Aid

I couldn't believe my eyes but there they were. Some of my elementary teachers were actually eating in the basement of my church. For a seven or eight year old, I found it amazing that teachers actually ate—and they were doing it in my church.

Well, why not? Once a month the Lutheran Church Ladies Aid would serve an evening meal for 20 cents and you could eat all of the tuna fish casserole and lime jello you wanted. It was a change of pace for many of the single school teachers who found the 20 cent price tag within their means.

This was one time my grandfather, **Rev. Eggers**, would get out of the way and let the ladies take over.

I'm surprised there is no reference to hot dishes or jello in scripture. Their power drew a lot of Watervillians to a church at least once a month. Hot dishes, lime jello and coffee have a lot to do with evangelism.

Muskrat Creek

We caught twelve muskrats that year and sold them to **Bob Rausch** for around $1.65 apiece. For three boys (**Joe Bittrich**, my brother, **Craig** and me) under 12 in 1955 that was a lot of money.

Muskrat Creek (the name we gave to it) flowed from the land belonging to **Robert Culhane, Sr.** north into Lake Tetonka (down the hill from where **Harold Preuss** lives). The creek wasn't over fifteen feet wide at any point but it was deep enough to have quite a few bank rats.

There was a lot of whooping and yelling that first morning we checked our traps and discovered our first muskrat.

My brother was the real trapper in the family. He would spend hours upon hours, days upon days, scouting **Robert Culhane's** woods and swamps and the southern shore of Lake Tetonka for good places to set his traps. I wasn't into trapping as much as he was but I used to follow along just to take in the smells of autumn and be part of his excitement and anticipation. There was nothing quite like autumn and trapping muskrats in Muskrat Creek.

Trapping Pigeons and revenge

Our cousin, **Bobby Raedeke,** got us started. I don't think there was anyone in Waterville that were as avid pigeon fanciers as **Craig** and I. We had a coop behind our place where my folks now live. We would get the pigeons by climbing among the rafters in barns at night and catch them with fish landing nets.

We transported them in gunny sacks and put them into our coop. After keeping them locked up and feeding them for a couple of weeks we would turn them loose to see them return to their new home.

To us, at the time, there was nothing as beautiful as seeing a flock of Homers, Baltimore Rollers, and Tumblers and ordinary barn pigeons flying through the sky.

And then the worst happened. Going out to feed them before school one winter morning, we discovered a large, black cat in the coop. Most of the twenty plus birds were inside the cat's stomach. The cat escaped—temporarily.

Then one day in the spring we saw the cat crossing the vacant lot near our home.

"Quick, get Dad's shotgun."

Dad's only shotgun at the time was a 16 gauge, Stevens double barrel with the stock engraved by **Marlowe Burns**. **Craig** let loose both barrels at about 30 yards and the cat went another ten and that was the end of the cat that ended the lives of our pigeons.

Revenge was never so sweet.

Spearing Northern Pike

I never saw a bigger northern than the one that one of our local politicians and **Craig** speared at **Osborn's** Dam around 1958. It must have weighted 20 plus pounds.

Spearing northerns was a spring ritual in Waterville for many boys and adults alike. The northerns would go up the creeks to spawn and the boys, with their dad's spears, would be waiting for them. Oh, we never got many, but our imaginations kept us in the game. Spearing northerns was something that was passed on from father to son. Fathers seemed to look the other way because their fathers looked the other way when they were young.

Whitewater Creek was the best and, probably, still is today—but I wouldn't know for sure.

HELP Wanted!

Men AND Women

Steady or Part Time

APPLY AT ONCE

We are authorized to use extra Farm help

Backman Produce Co.

Waterville, Minn.

All teenagers are invited to attend a party on Friday evening from 8:00-10:30 at the Legion Hall. (1957)

Swiping Watermelons

Raiding someone's watermelon patch was never a sin to me. I came to the conclusion that Waterville residents purposely raised watermelons to keep teenage boys off of the streets. For all we knew it was part of Waterville's summer recreation program.

Swiping melons was akin to shooting a bean shooter in school or putting wax on windows during Halloween. It was part of the rites of passage—just don't get caught and be careful of the birdshot.

When the northerns began making their way up Whitewater Creek in the spring, it was only natural that you went out and tried to spear a few. When the watermelons began to ripen in the fall, it was only natural that you would go out and try to swipe a few.

It's interesting that the kids who raided the watermelon patches never used the word "steal." It was always swipe or raid.

Well the best patches were on the north side. **"Gregors"** and **"Goltz's"** had outstanding examples of watermelons.

We would walk the tracks east of the swimming beach, hop down in the patch located on the east side of the tracks in the back yard of the owner, grab a few and run north along the tracks. When we got to the trestle, we would stop and inspect our pickings. Rarely, did we get one that was red ripe. But we didn't care, the fun was in the "gettin" and not the "eatin."

Who were the thieves? In my time there was myself and my brother (actually, I kind of tagged along), **Bob Grobe, Bill Norman, Ray Bremer, Leon Mager, Dale Campbell, David Rosenau** and maybe a few others).

That was the north side patch. On the west side of town there was **Al Kinrod's** patch and a few others. My brother and I, **Joe Bittrich, Clarence Harriman, Robert Scholer**, to name a few, were the thieves on this side of town.

There were other gangs in town that performed this ritual. Of course there were always rumors about someone getting shot with birdshot. It could have happened but it never made the papers.

Halloween

To this day, I don't know who did it. We (**Joey Bittrich, Craig** and myself) were standing in the vicinity of what used to be **Pete Solyntjes** market on Halloween night. We may have just come out of the bowling alley where we had gone to get some treats. A good size bucket of water drenched the three of us from the second floor. It was a big laugh to the people standing around—but not to us. Later, it made for a good story. I remember having damp clothes on a cool evening and a soggy bag of candy.

Halloween in Waterville was the best of times. With our masks on (we didn't go in for costumes) we would visit the houses in West Waterville and work our way downtown to visit the bars and businesses. The bars were the best because every now and then you would get a quarter.

Most candy wasn't wrapped and you often got cookies, popcorn balls and apples. By the time you were home everything had a popcorn flavor to it and was in a big wad of cookie, candy and popcorn—but still edible.

Outhouses were still around and many would be on their sides by morning—but not by us. We were good little boys and we may have waxed a few windows but that was the extent of our tricks. However, had we known the name of the person who gave us the Halloween bath, another outhouse may have been tipped over.

Lake Tetonka, Waterville, Minn. ROCKY POINT 1913

Harold Hebl is the president of the recently formed education association. (1952)

Christmas Pageants

There are Christmas programs and there are Christmas pageants. Pageants were major productions where elementary teachers would rehearse their students for weeks before Christmas vacation. Then in one Friday evening, it was over.

To be part of the Christmas pageant was a real honor. Because there was only one section per grade, most kids were in the pageant. I can recall being a gnome one year and a reader another time.

They were performed on the stage in the old high school. Moms would make the costumes. There would be standing room only in the gym. Without any microphone system, I'm surprised anyone heard us.

The excitement and anticipation of the pageant was about as much as I could handle. They were a great prelude to the best thing about Christmas. After the pageant you could look forward to two weeks of furlough from school.

Dances and Sock Hops

This was the age of rock and roll and this new and different music became a big part of the lives of teens in the fifties. We played the music in our cars, on our transistor radios, and on the juke boxes in **Jacobson's** Red Top Cafe, **Richard Wong's** OK Cafe and **Larsons** Cafe. Although it was never officially documented, I probably had the biggest and best collection of 45's in the city. **Bob Grobe** might argue that.

I'm not sure where it all started. It could have been in 1956 when Elvis sang "Hound Dog" on the Ed Sullivan show that came on at 7:00 on Sunday evenings. It also could have started with Dick Clark's Bandstand that came on at 4:00 every afternoon. In any event, rock and roll provided the background music for growing up.

A lot of dances were held in the schools after the football and basketball games. Dances were also held at the Elysian Community Hall and at your friends' parties.

I have to admit that in order to maintain my "macho" image, I wasn't a dancer. Imagine a gym full of kids, kids sitting on the bleachers, girls dancing with girls, some boys dancing with girls and a lot of boys holding up the walls around the gym. I was a wall holder.

Santo and Johnny, Dion, Buddy Holly, they were all there. The lights were dim and your mind took excursions into *Blue Moon*. You wished you were out there on the dance floor doing the kinds of things they did on Bandstand but. . .

It was tough getting boys to dance. Physical education teacher **George Barnard** had a student teacher one time that tried to teach dancing. It was the only time that I can recall our physical education classes being coed. Well, this first time teacher did her best and as I recall she was a pretty good teacher but I wasn't cooperating too well so she booted me out. **Mr. Barnard** motioned for me to go to the study hall that **Mr. Dahl** happened to have. When I told him I was kicked out, he kind of smiled and motioned me to take a seat.

Well, if I could do anything over again during the 50's it would be to have one last dance.

That why I dig rock and roll music any ol' way you use it. It's got to be rock and roll music if you want to dance with me.

SHOES
LOOK LIKE NEW
when repaired by
GUS HINZ

First House south of
Fahning Supply Co.

"Buc the Birds"
WATERVILLE
HOMECOMING
Oct. 7, 1955

"The race" — Last day of school

There were several reasons why I looked forward to the last day of school during my elementary years.

It represented the best of times. Picnic, games, and the chance to walk over to the football field, which, at that time, seemed miles away from the school. Kids would try to out do each other to see who brought the best lunch.

The race was my opportunity to uphold my reputation of being the fastest runner. There would be a race among the girls and among the boys. I would be anxious about the race for several weeks before the event—wondering if I would come in first again. It seemed that nothing was more important to me than coming in first—and I did, every year for six years. (I was always thankful that **Mary Roemhildt** and **Vicky Meyers** raced with the girls because I think they would have beaten any of the boys).

As special as winning the race was to me, the picnic signaled the last day of school that signaled the first day of vacation. In the movie *Field of Dreams*, Shoeless Joe Jackson asks Kevin Costner, "Is this heaven?"

Kevin Costner replies, "No, this is Iowa."

If some one were to ask me on the first day school was out if this was heaven, I would have said, "Yes."

John Dickie graduated "Cum Laude" in chemistry from the University of Minnesota. (1956)

Finally we were free, free to do anything we wanted for three solid months. Swimming, fishing, hiking, camping, going out to my uncle's farm, going to the Waseca Fair, hiking around Lake Tetonka, catching pigeons, lighting off fire crackers, movies, card parties, playing football, catching night crawlers—if heaven turns out to be like summer vacation in the late forties and fifties, it's going to be great.

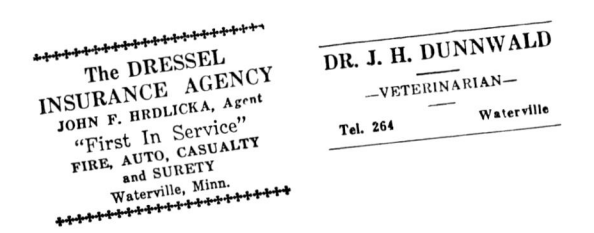

```
The DRESSEL              DR. J. H. DUNNWALD
INSURANCE AGENCY         —VETERINARIAN—
JOHN F. HRDLICKA, Agent
"First In Service"       Tel. 264        Waterville
FIRE, AUTO, CASUALTY
and SURETY
Waterville, Minn.
```

May Basket Day

I didn't do it intentionally although now that I think of it, I could have. Tradition held that when you placed a May basket on a girl's doorstep and if she saw you do it, she would chase you, catch you and kiss you. Well, when I put my May basket on **Mary Roemhildt's** doorstep, apparently she was not home because I escaped—for the moment.

Later in the day, I went to answer our door and there stood **Mary**. Before I knew it she was chasing me down the lawn during a fairly heavy rain. As fate would have it, she caught me and, yes, kissed me. Come to think of it, I probably slipped on the wet grass. That was the first and last time I was kissed in the rain on May Basket Day.

Scouts

When **Leona Anderson** was our Cub Scout troop leader we carved things out of Ivory soap. When **Jim Backman** was our scoutmaster, we went camping on the west side of Fish Lake.

I can remember the night the Tenderfoot scouts were initiated. **Dr. Rieke**, Scoutmaster, and the other scouts blindfolded us and took us out to the Mile Bridge, now Sakatah State Park. I recall eating coffee grounds and orange peel and being paddled once or twice.

Thanks to people like **Dr. Rieke, Jim Backman,** my dad and **Jerry Jewel** and with people like **Betty Schulz** with the Girl Scouts, scouting has always been an important part of Waterville. For me it was just another thing to do that was fun and I even learned a few things about the outdoors. I think our dues were five cents a week.

Adventure at Dusbabek's Market

The friendly atmosphere of **Dusbabek's** Market was one reason why you would go in there. **Frank Dusbabek** and son, **Bob**, always wore smiles.

Area hunting parties bringing their deer into **Dusbabek's** for butchering was the second reason. Deer weren't as plentiful in southern Minnesota as they are today and to see a line up of deer, well you didn't forget about it for a few days and it was something to look forward to next year.

What a sight! For a boy of 7 or 8, to see all of those northern Minnesota deer hanging in a southern Minnesota grocery store cooler was an adventure. Of course you always heard a story or two and that was part of the cooler experience.

Well, that was **Dusbabek's**—friendly people and a bunch of deer in the cooler. Before everyone owned a freezer, they would also rent out freezer space. My dad took advantage of this benefit. I think he did it just to entertain us so we could look at the deer hanging in **Dusbabek's** cooler. It was worth it.

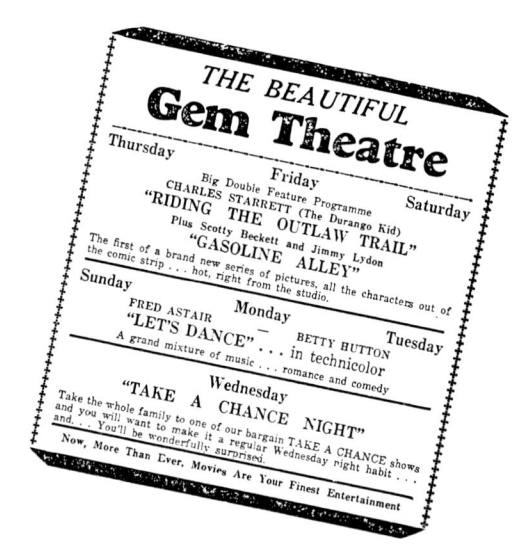

```
THE BEAUTIFUL
Gem Theatre
Thursday                              Saturday
          Big Double Feature Programme
          CHARLES STARRETT (The Durango Kid)
              Friday
          "RIDING THE OUTLAW TRAIL"
          Plus Scotty Beckett and Jimmy Lydon
              "GASOLINE ALLEY"
          The first of a brand new series of pictures, all the characters out of
          the comic strip... hot, right from the studio.
Sunday       Monday              Tuesday
FRED ASTAIR               BETTY HUTTON
    "LET'S DANCE"... in technicolor
    A grand mixture of music... romance and comedy
              Wednesday
          "TAKE A CHANCE NIGHT"
          Take the whole family to one of our bargain TAKE A CHANCE shows
          and you will want to make it a regular Wednesday night habit...
          and... You'll be wonderfully surprised.
          Now, More Than Ever, Movies Are Your Finest Entertainment
```

The Gem Theatre

My parents would give my brother and me 15 cents each to go to the movies during the late 40's and 50's. With the cost of the movie being nine cents (I have no idea why it was such an odd amount) we would have six cents left in change.

Our next task would be to go around and ask other movie goers for the penny they received in change. When we obtained four more we could buy a box of popcorn for 10 cents. If we didn't get it, my brother would settle for a roll of *Reed's* winter green life savers and I would buy a box of *Dots* or *Spearmint Leaves*.

There was a ritual in going to the movies. We always sat in the same seats. **Craig** had the aisle seat in the first row, **Joey Bittrich** had the second from the aisle, and I had the third seat from the aisle. When **Dennis Bittrich** joined us later he sat next to me on the left. **Mr. Cameron's** son, **Bob**, had the center seat in the first row—always.

We would always get there about fifteen minutes before the movie started. I don't know why. For some strange reason we thought someone would want our seats.

The beautiful Gem was where most people in Waterville first heard classical music because **Mr. Cameron** played it before the movie began.

Friday night movies meant there was usually a western showing. There were also a cartoon, a news reel, a short film and the previews of upcoming attractions. Local merchants also had commercials—especially car dealers.

On the way home from the movie, we would talk about it and reenact some of the scenes. Since every cowboy movie was virtually the same, we got to be pretty good stand ins. But, alas, we were never discovered—at least, not yet.

The interesting thing about our movie going was that our parents never went with us. We were seven or eight at the time; we walked there and returned in the dark. Terrible things never happened in small communities—except the time that Marlon Brando in *The Waterfront* said "damn," now that was terrible. Or, was it "he" double toothpicks?

```
ARTHUR F. SCHEID
ATTORNEY-AT-LAW
General Practice—Probating and
Collections
Office and Res. 437 East Main St.
Waterville, Minnesota
```

Friday Night Football:

On frosty fall evenings my father would take my brother and me to the Waterville football games. Gosh, I can remember it as if it were yesterday. There would be our heroes: **Bob Bittrich, Hank Bittrich, Tommy Rohrer, Carl Adams, Ross Ellingworth.**

While the big guys were playing on the field, the little guys were playing on the hill just west of the field. By the time the game ended we were just as sweaty as our heroes.

Sometimes an amazing thing would happen that would seemingly bring not only our playing to a stop but also the playing on the field. The coaches, the fans, the players would look up in the dark, star filled sky and listen and listen to hear the sounds of the geese. We would gaze hard through the darkness to see their "V" formation moving south.

There is nothing in the world that could match the sound of the geese. And then the honking and crying would fade and the games would go on.

Klondike Hill:

Although it's not in Waterville, I talk as if it were or is. Klondike Hill or Jesse James Hill was the only landmark people who didn't know about Waterville might be impressed with. When talking to strangers, we always used to say, "And Jesse James stopped at the big hill near Waterville as a hide out. You probably didn't know that."

Actually the hill was closer to Elysian but somehow the people in Waterville claimed rights to the hill and the story.

As the story goes, the Jesse James gang came through Waterville after he robbed the Northfield Bank September 7, 1876 and hid out on Klondike Hill. It was the highest hill around and it served as a lookout for the posse.

I hiked on Klondike several times and always imagined myself finding a pistol to verify the story. "Waterville boy finds pistol belonging to Jesse James." It may still be there.

What is certain is that the gang did stop at the Waterville House located on the corner of the old Gem Theatre on their way to Northfield. Personally the Klondike Hill story is still my favorite.

Dr. Rieke's office

The stairs are still there and every time I walk past them I think of how many times I climbed them to keep my appointment with **Dr. Lowell Rieke**, local dentist.

I don't think there was a man in Waterville that was more respected than **"Doc" Rieke**. He was a good dentist and an exceptional citizen.

The students dreaded those pink dental cards when they were distributed each fall. They meant that you had to have them signed by a dentist, which meant that you had to have your teeth checked, which meant you might have a cavity. In the days of no fluoride, I, for one, always had a cavity or two.

Doc always had a smile on his face and tried to get you to smile in spite of the fact you had to face the dreaded drill. **Doc** had a lot of compassion for people although sometimes it was hard for him to show it with a drill in his hand.

As I walk past those stairs I feel there should be a plaque over the doorway that says, "These stairs led to the office of **Doctor Lowell Rieke**, a distinguished citizen of Waterville."

```
DR. L. L. RIEKE
DENTIST
Office Buesgens Bldg., Lake Street
Tel. 251          Waterville
```

Seining fish at Osborn's Dam

Both Lake Tetonka and Sakatah were notorious for their supply of rough fish.

Seeing the carp and buffalo fish swarm in the fish trap located under the Cannon River bridge at the outlet of Lake Tetonka in the spring was a great show.

Citizen of the week was Tom Broughton, father of Irene Greer. (1950)

The fish hatchery people, led by **Rollie Ruths**, would make a trap out of willow branches that the fish could swim through but could not escape. They would be trapped in a corral made out of snow fence.

There would always be cars stopped by the bridge to look at the fish. And there was the usual talk of someone seeing a huge northern or walleye in the trap.

On the day the men would come and empty the trap there would be standing room only. It was quite a sight. The guys would bring their nets to round up the fish in the trap and throw them in boxes. The game fish would be returned to the lake.

Some people would say we fed the entire city of Chicago. And, we probably did because many of the fish seined from our lakes ended up in Chicago.

Fish Lake Woods

Imagine a late sunny September morning when the leaves are beginning to fall from the trees and the sunlight dances its way through the yellow and red leaves on the maple and oak trees. Dad would drop my brother and me off at the woods west of Lake Tetonka on the **John Roessler** farm. We would spend the day squirrel hunting with Dad's Remington bolt action rifle.

There was no thought of tomorrow—only this moment mattered. Walking through Fish Lake Woods in the autumn was a great lesson in nature appreciation. I'll never forget it.

A game warden story

There's the Jesse James story, the story about a fourteen foot sturgeon in Lake Tetonka, and then there is the game warden story—only this one is true. In 1940 **Bryant Baumgarten**, who operated a fish market, got into some trouble with game wardens over the fish limits. Three game wardens came to see **Baumgarten** and to check to see that he wasn't doing anything illegal. They kept pestering him so much that he finally cracked. Before any of the three game wardens could do anything **Baumgarten** had used a shotgun on all three. After shooting the game wardens he went behind a truck and shot himself. There were four witnesses: **Charles Coon, Art Francisco, Edward Vail, and Linden Vail**. The shooting gave Waterville a bad reputation for a long time.

First TV and Farmer Marlin

The **Walter Bittrich** home in our neighborhood was one of the first to acquire a television. Farmer Marlin was his name and professional wrestling was his game. It was a popular program and it was the first TV program I saw. For days after, **Joe Bittrich**, my brother **Craig** and I would play professional wrestling on the lawn and execute his famous "mule kick."

Professional wrestling was made popular by television. It was so popular there was an occasional match in the high school gym. At one of these matches held in the early 50's, they advertised that for the first time ever, a man would wrestle a woman. They did and I was there to see it. As I recall it was rather a boring match.

The Narrows

To this day, the Narrows is one of my favorite spots in Waterville. I associate it with the stories my dad tells about the pass shooting for ducks he and **Glenn Preuss** engaged in. Driving to the narrows and looking for ducks a couple of weeks before the opening of duck season remains a thrilling experience for me. The trip conjures up all sorts of expectancies for opening day.

Near the Narrows was located Wood Tick Hollow--everyone's lover's lane. Hardly a night went by when there wasn't a car or two or three parked there—so I am told.

Night Crawlers

Ward's Resort (located where **Wilme's** Resort was) paid one cent per night crawler—alive. Fertilizers and weed killers were not used on lawns in the 50's so you could always count on finding lots of fat crawlers after a rain. Today's crawler catchers know that it takes a quick hand and a good back. Catching night crawlers became a nice source of revenue for young boys who believed that being rich started after 50 cents.

Ice Wagon

Sawdust isn't so bad when it is surrounded by clear, cold ice and a 90 degree July day. Many families still used the ice box for refrigeration in the late 40's. To this day, I often refer to the refrigerator as the ice box.

Tom Broughton's ice wagon was a welcome sight on those hot days. Sometimes he was the Pied Piper as kids would follow the

Mrs. Pete Solyntjes died. John Frodl was married in Minneapolis. (1940)

wagon and get a chip of ice to suck on. Even though ice was frozen lake water that was packed in **Carl Stavenau's** ice house, I don't recall anyone ever getting sick from eating too much of it.. The Lake Sakatah advocates would probably say, "Well that's because the ice was from Lake Sakatah. Our water is much cleaner."

Mrs. Pischel

Bertha Pischel was quite a woman. She was one of the workers at the **Andrews** Opera House on the north side of Lake Tetonka. She also posed as Santa Claus and on more than one occasion dropped around on Christmas Eve to bring my brother and me a cookie. She was a great cook and people would often ask her for her recipes. My mother says she was happy to give them out but would leave out an ingredient or two. She took pride in her cooking.

A couple of years after **Kathy** and I married, we purchased her square oak dining room table and chairs for $65. We still use the chairs.

She drove an old Chevy to town to do her shopping and always had trouble starting it because it used the outside crank. When she shopped at the Red Owl, **Don O'Brien** always went out and started her car for her. No wonder she shopped at Red Owl. Another reason she shopped there was she would ask me (when I worked at Red Owl) to go over to the Corner Bar and buy her a pint of apricot brandy. She said she needed it on those cold winter nights. And now everyone knows your secret for longevity, **Bertha**. Rest in peace.

Doug Grover

Whenever a town loses one of its young people, it hurts. Waterville hurt a lot in 1957 when **Doug Grover** was killed in a car accident during the week of the Waterville Centennial celebration. **Doug Grover** was an outstanding athlete and person. He was an idol and role model for younger Waterville boys like myself.

The Waterville High School Memorial Trophy given out to Waterville High School's best athletes was a tribute to **Doug's** character and ability.

I remember **Doug Grover** very vividly on account of one particular instance. It happened when I was in 7th grade. My friends said they were going to try out for baseball and I followed. One of the first days of practice was one of my last days. **Coach Barnard** was having us do some batting practice in the new gym. **Doug Grover**, a high school junior at the time, was pitching. I saw the ball coming but froze. An instant later the ball bounced off of my jaw.

Surprisingly, I was OK. Both **Doug** and **Coach Barnard** showed a lot of compassion to the hit ball player. Alas, I became a track person and probably for the better. Actually, to tell my friends that I was hit by a **Doug Grover** pitched ball and lived to tell about it was an honor.

Fires

I suppose it was because Waterville had a volunteer fire department but one of the greatest thrills for a young boy was seeing the parade of cars follow the fire trucks. It was a three ring circus. Not only did the volunteer firemen follow the trucks but it seemed as if the whole town did as well.

When there was a fire, the firemen would drop whatever they were doing and go. The phone operators would some how track them down and tell them the whereabouts of the fire. The siren would blow in town, the truck would head out and the people would follow. We're talking major excitement for a small town. After awhile reports would filter back as to where it was and what happened.

The Waterville firefighters took their jobs seriously. I recently learned that firefighting ranks number one on the most dangerous professions list. The men always had a great deal of respect from Waterville citizens. Now you know why.

Jim Rohl's barbershop:

Jim was always whistling. I can't recall him ever being in a sour mood. He took a real and sincere interest in his customers. He always had questions to ask you about school and sports.

Because the chair was for adults, he would put a padded board over the armrests and set me on the board until I was big enough to sit in the chair.

Maurice Enghausen will have charge of senior high English and Speech instruction at WHS. (1957)

Scene at Lake Sakatah — Waterville - Minn

Haircuts were fifty cents. My dad would always stop to pay after work. People were trusting.

Those were the days of Vaseline Hair Oil and Wildroot Cream Oil—both guaranteed not to give you the dry hair look. I was a Vaseline man. There was so much alcohol in it that it stung your scalp when it was applied. No wonder I never had head lice.

Jim always had a good supply of comics to read. I suppose **Jim** was as much a contributor to my learning to read as were the schools.

There were three barbers in town during the 40's, 50's and 60's. **Jim Rohl, Walt Schulz** (east of **Jim's** and in the basement), and **Snub Novalosky** who was below the Security State Bank. Selecting your barber was kind of like selecting your church. Once you made your selection, you stayed.

Creativity was not a major part of the barber business. You could choose from three cuts: the regular, the heine, and the flat-top.

My parents said they always had a good time with **Jim** and **Chris.**. They were good people.

Waterville's airport

The first time I flew in an airplane was with **Jim Rohl**. In 1945 **Jim, Cleve Cram, John Sheldon, and Ed Goltz** took flying lessons. Their airport was the lake and the lessons were sponsored by Vogel's Creamery. **Margaret Goltz** said if **Ed** was going to fly, she would too. And she did. Happy landing, **Margaret**.

Bob's old car

When our neighbor **Bob Bittrich** got his old '37 Chevrolet, it was a contest to see how many kids he could pack into it to take to school on those cold winter mornings. And what a thrill it was for us little guys to ride with a high school student. High school students represented heroes to young kids and **Bob** was one of them.

Pot Luck Bunch

The pot luck bunch was as much a part of my family as my regular family. **Harriet** and **Jack Backman, Earl** and **Annie Fritz, Irma** and **Harold Kopiscke, Molly** and **Glenn Preuss, Harold** and **Grace Preuss, Mabel** and **Bob Rausch, Peg** and **Al Roeglin,** and **Sylvia** and **Art Roeglin**. Often this group would be joined by **Vi** and **Al Comeaux**. The children were also a big part of the regular family: **Gene** and **Randy Preuss, Gretchen, Jennifer, Rhonda,** and **Sara Jane Rausch, Bobby** and **Janice Roeglin, Cathy Fritz, Sally, Kathy, Elizabeth Backman** and **Craig** and **me.**

I'm not sure how the Pot Luck Bunch got started but there was hardly a month and sometimes a week that went by when there wasn't a gathering at someone's home. Members of the group would hunt and fish together, go to Iowa/Minnesota games, and play cards. There was always a lot of fun to be had at the gatherings and a lot to eat. The Pot Luck Bunch was quite a bunch.

Sportsman's Club trap shoots

The leaves are about ready to turn colors, there is a certain coolness in the air and the farmers are preparing to go into the fields to harvest. And, the Waterville hunters are preparing for the hunting season.

We knew hunting season was upon us when the Waterville Sportsman Club would sponsor the Sunday trap shoot at the Club House

Dennis Bittrich is getting along nicely following an operation on an ear one day last week. (1956)

on the west end of Lake Tetonka. **Glenn Preuss, Jack Backman, Art Roeglin, Bob Rausch, Edgar Eggers, Paul Schulz, Al Comeaux, Dr. Rieke, Bob Sherratt, Fritz Taylor, Bob Buckmaster, Don Clemens** are just a few of the Waterville sportsmen who would shoot a couple of boxes of shells each Sunday at the clay pigeons that would fly from the cement block building.

It was the job of the kids to go out into the lake to find any that had not been hit. Because the west end of the lake is sandy and shallow for quite a ways out, we were able to gently feel the unbroken pigeons with our feet. There was always a contest to see who could find the most unbroken ones.

The Sunday trap shoots in the fifties were just one of many Waterville traditions that made fall my favorite time of the year.

Take a Chance Night At the Gem

Every Wednesday night at the beautiful Gem Theatre was "Take a Chance" night. The titles weren't announced until the lights were off and the curtains opened. One of the best movies I remember seeing was the *Lou Goehrig Story* starring Gary Cooper. I went to the movie on that particular evening with **Grandma Raedeke (Grannie Alma)** who I was spending the night with. On the way home we had to cross the railroad tracks at the junction of Reed and Main Streets. It was in the summer and it was still light at about 9:00 in the evening. There was a train going north on the tracks and it was about even with **Fritz Taylor's** junk yard located a block to the south. My grandma stopped at the crossing to wait until the train passed. Being a lad of about eight and quick (and foolish), I let go of my grandma's hand and dashed across the tracks to hear the whistle of the train cross behind me. That was the first time and only time I recall that I felt the wrath of my **Grannie Alma**. But, what did she expect? It was take a chance night.

Cards: The hidden curriculum

I know why kids didn't get into a lot of trouble in the fifties. They were too busy playing cards. I find it hard to believe that anyone could grow up in Waterville without having a pretty good understanding of at least three or four card games. I still believe that the game of *Snouse* originated in the Waterville/Elysian area because I never knew anyone outside the area who knew how to play it. If we didn't play Snouse, we played *Crazy Eights, Spoon, Casino, Cribbage, Hearts, Canasta* or *"Oh, Hell."*

Cards always came easy for me. I have this sneaky suspicion that being able to find success at cards is hereditary. My mother is great at cards and plays *Bridge* in her sleep.

My brother and I played *Canasta* with the Rausch girls, *Crazy Eights* with the Pot Luck Bunch kids, *Snouse* with our German relatives and friends, *Cribbage* with my Uncle **Roy Raedeke** and neighbor **Jack Backman** and *Casino* with **Grannie Alma**. Some of our best games happened in the summer after we would play football on **Linden Ebling's** vacant lot near our home in west Waterville. We would go to the cool of our basement and either play *Hearts* or *"Oh, Hell."* **Leon Mager, Jr., Ray Bremer, Dave Rosenau, Leon Nesbitt, Jr., Paul Prahl, Bob Grobe, Bob Culhane, Bill Norman** are just a few of the kids that I used to beat regularly.

Dave Rosenau and I played a *Cribbage* tournament during our entire freshman year at Luther College. At the end we were tied and each of us had won well over a hundred games. Dave may tell it differently, but I think I was the one who won the last and deciding game. What could you expect from someone with cards in their blood?

Ruth Grover, Duane Roemhildt, June Nushbaum and Jeannette Prehn are the cast in a play presented to the P.T.A.. (1956)

Fishing Bullheads:

Few of Waterville's founding fathers would have believed that the bullhead would be the thing to put Waterville on the map. What would the neighbors think? Well the neighbors must have thought it was a good idea because it's Waterville's neighbors that keeps Waterville on the map. The founding fathers of Waterville are still turning over in their graves. To think that its future generation would sell its soul to a bullhead.

There is an unwritten law in Waterville that in order to live there you have to like bullheads and eat them at least once a year. There is more than one Watervillian that is "bullheaded." Do you think there is any connection?

Well, fishing bullheads was a spring ritual. They often bit the best in the evening—after dark. We would cast our lines from the shore near **Osborn's** Bridge and let the night crawler and sinker rest on the bottom. When the tips on our rods began to move we would grab them and give a jerk to set the hook. No wonder my father is such a great bullhead cleaner—he had a lot of practice cleaning ours.

Dave Rosenau and I caught 44 huge yellow bellies one time while sitting on **Glenn Preuss'** dock while casting into a cold north wind blowing waves and white caps onto the rocky shore. I think we became official Waterville citizens on that day.

Popcorn Wagon:

The best kept secret in Minnesota was and still is the Waterville popcorn wagon. You can get the largest size bag of popcorn for the least money anywhere in the 50 states. It's difficult to pass the wagon (now a stationary building) without buying a bag. Loaded with butter and coming with conversation from its owner, **Darlene Courtney Hoban,** it is part of Waterville's marvelous traditions. The wagon was previously owned by **Lil Michaels**.

> READ WATERVILLE AREA NEWS FIRST IN THE ADVANCE
> SHOP at your LOCAL STORE
> Your only COMPLETE source of local news
>
> jack webster's...
> SPORTS CORNER

Waterville City Dump

Every time I took a trip to the Waterville city dump, I would picture myself in some science fiction movie where a planet had been over run by rodents and there was nothing remaining but smoldering debris. I enjoyed going to the city dump (located on the north side of the highway across from the high school baseball field) once or twice a week with my father to dispose of our garbage. Sometimes brother and I would ride out there on our bikes. We always found something interesting to see. On one occasion my father found an old oak ice box that he took home and refinished.

Elmer Geyer used to be the caretaker there for many years. He would make sure that things got burned and that people dumped things in the right place. I miss the old dump. I suppose a couple centuries from now archeologists will conduct a dig over the old dump site and with the artifacts they will open a museum. They might find someone's old hula-hoop and wonder what it was used for.

American Bandstand

It started every day at 4:00 in the late 50's and for one hour most teens in Waterville would hurry home from school to catch Dick Clark hosting America's most popular rock and roll record hop—*American Bandstand*. Danny and the Juniors, Fabian, Frankie Avalon, and Connie Francis—they were all there in your own home. The "do-wop," "sha-na-na-na" and other "be-bop" sounds would take you away from Waterville and carry you on to the dance floor with the Bandstand regulars. For the next 24 hours we would stroll to its tunes until it was time for *Bandstand* again: *where the music was upbeat and the sounds were great—Bandstand.*

High School

The thing I looked forward to every year when school began was the smell of the building. It was a combination of an antiseptic, locker room, lunch room, classroom smell. It was unique to the Waterville school. When I graduated in 1961, it was the smell I missed the most and it's probably the reason I became a teacher. I've learned that every school has its own unique smell—kind of a comforting smell.

I don't think I learned much in high school, at least the stuff found in textbooks. And, my grades showed it. I did have a lot of respect for my teachers: **Mr. Kelly, Mr. Dahl, Mr. Bengston, Mr. Barnard, Mrs. Sautbine, Mr. Enghausen, Mr. Mesken, Mr. Wilkes** and **Mr. Bohn.** I even liked **Miss Bishop** in a special way. She knew where the animal books were found in the library. They were good people.

I don't think I ever did formally thank my teachers. Most students don't. I better say, "thank you" now. They may expect a free book.

Craig and John Eggers score six touchdowns as Waterville beats Belle Plaine 65-0. (1958)

The Red Top Cafe: Waterville's Rec Center

During my junior and senior years (1959-1961) at WHS, the Red Top Cafe was my cafeteria. My parents would give me 25 cents for lunch. With that 25 cents I could get a hamburger and a coke or a hamburger and one of **Glenn's** jelly bismarks with white frosting.

A cherry coke was ten cents and a mudball cost about 15 cents. The twenty cent hamburgers were great. There were a couple of pin ball machines and rack of 25 cent pulp novels like *High School Confidential*, *Blackboard Jungle*, and *Teen Tramp*.

But the Red Top was more than a cafe. It was Waterville's teen center. It was run by the **Jacobson's**. **Delores**, the daughter, was a classmate. The Red Top was the place where teens met after school, after dances, after football and basketball games. It had the jukebox and Chuck Berry and the Chiffons. It had everything a teen could want.

That Football Feeling

It's a cool October evening. The Buccaneers begin to enter the locker room around six o'clock. There isn't too much talking, some clowning, but not too much.

We begin to put on our clean white and green football uniforms. We gather in the wrestling room. Coach **Dahl** and Coach **Kelly** come in and talk to us. They give us some last minute advice.

The captains lead us up the cement stairs. You hear the fiber glass or aluminum cleats on the polished floors as the players cross the floor to the stairs and out the south doors of the old high school.

We have our helmets under our arms and as we walk across the dirt playground, we see the lights of the field and begin to hear the murmuring of the crowd and the cries of the cheerleaders. We approach the cyclone fence surrounding the football field, put on our helmets, begin yelling our war cry and are led onto the field by the captains.

The grass is wet with the evening dew, the air is cool and fresh, our breath rushes out in a white mist, we smell the night and everything is the way it ought to be.

Freshman Initiation

There was a time at Waterville High School when freshmen were initiated. By the time I became a freshman, the rites had been toned down considerably. I recall when freshmen like **Jerome Nusbaum, Mary Ann Walz, Carl Adams, Jim Ayres, Judy Carlson, Gary Dusbabek, Wally Murker, Ken Weilage, Duane Roemhildt** and **Karen Greer** and others had to dress in gunny sacks, wear necklaces of garlic, and were paraded through the streets of Waterville. Now that was an initiation.

Our initiation took place in the old gym and each of us had to do something crazy. I know we had to wear our shirts backwards and I had to pretend that I was Jayne Mansfield. **Vicky Meyers** had to pick up hundreds of BB's that had been dropped on the gym floor—good clean fun.

Those times have gone but the various rites of passage that kids were subjected to probably helped us more than they harmed us. The adults kind of looked the other way because they knew how important revenge was for the sophomore class that administered the initiation rites.

Rocky Point

This was my favorite place. How many times had I sat on the hill near Rocky Point overlooking Lake Tetonka, I can't tell you. But every time I did, I always came away feeling a little better.

The Rocky Point woods and surrounding area that was owned by **Bob Culhane** had eveything—rabbits, mink, raccoon, muskrat, pheasants, squirrels, and even an occasional deer. For my brother and I, it was our favorite get away.

Rocky Point was also a favorite place for my mother and father. My father took this photo of our family in the 1940's on Rocky Point hill. It was a spring day, trees were budding and my father probably suggested we go on a picnic.

In my younger days I had carved the initials of a childhood sweetheart on a tree on Rocky Point hill. The tree is gone, houses have replaced the hill, but the memories and good times I had at Rocky Point overlooking Lake Tetonka will always remain with me.

Craig, John and Helen Eggers at Rocky Point - 1945

The Girl Scouts are taking orders for birthday calendars. Call Marge Bohn if you are interested at 232. (1960)

Greetings From Waterville, Minn.

A look into the future
Waterville: 2096

If you were to visit Waterville in the year 2096 you would discover one startling fact—nothing had changed. On the contrary, it was exactly the way **John R. Eggers** had described it in his 1996 book, *Greetings From Waterville, Minn.*

In the year 2057, at Waterville's 200 year birthday, the citizens of Waterville became uneasy with the direction it had taken over the past fifty years. People were beginning to refer to the Waterville area as the Minne-Wa-Wa connection—Minneapolis-Waterville-Waseca. It was becoming increasingly difficult to determine where one city began and the other city left off. Waterville's independence was being squeezed from the north and from the south. They didn't like it.

In some ways Waterville had become the Wisconsin Dells of Southern Minnesota. People came to Waterville to have their picture taken in front of 30 foot tall Barney, Betty and Little Barney Bullhead. The Bullhead ride in the amusement park located where the Phil Mart station was located had become a "don't miss" attraction.

Whereas Waterville had become a commercial mecca to the joy of its founding fathers, there was something missing. And then one day some "music men" came to Waterville to make the citizens an offer they couldn't refuse—in exchange for their souls.

Representatives of a conglomerate made a pitch to the City Council that should they accept their offer, the citizens of Waterville would become millionaires overnight. They proposed to buy the entire city, both lakes including the State Park and all of the land within a five mile radius. (The State Parks had been turned over to the cities in 2020 when they became too costly for the State to run.)

Watervillians had a difficult decision to make. They could

Mr. and Mrs. Chester Miller had as their guests for dinner, Mr. and Mrs. Robert Slattery and sons. (1959)

Greetings From Waterville, Minn.

give away the keys to their city and live on easy street the rest of their lives or they could continue as is. They chose neither.

After considerable debate including much discussion of what the citizens of Waterville valued most and what they remembered from their parents and grandparents, not only did they choose not to take the conglomerate's offer they proposed to do something that had never been done before.

FREE coon feed
Tuesday, Nov. 19
EVERYONE INVITED

Waterville Bar
WATERVILLE, MINN.

From that moment on until the task was completed in 2096, Watervillians turned back the clock and began an unprecedented restoration. It was as if someone had placed a bubble over the entire area and once you entered the bubble, you took a "bunny hop" step into the 1950's.

For forty years Watervillians worked hard to restore Waterville to its 1950 look. It became the first totally 50's community in the United States. Within a five mile radius of Waterville, homes, farms, factories, churches, schools, businesses and banks were transformed into an era that featured 1950 Fords, flat top haircuts, and forty five RPM records.

When word got around about what Waterville was attempting to do, it became America's dream city. *Time* and *Newsweek* featured Waterville on their covers. *Time* magazine voted the citizens of Waterville as People of the Year for not going with the flow and for swimming up stream. Whereas the rest of the world rode the waves of technology, one small city and surrounding countryside decided to stop the clock and become a living history of life as it once was.

Visitors would be picked up five miles from the center of town and driven in 1950's autos. From the center of the city they could choose to visit farms like the **Henry Fessel** Farm, fish bullheads with a steel rod and black line at the Narrows or **Osborn's** dam, or camp in tents or trailers at Sakatah Park or Kamp **Dels** and enjoy a camp fire. They could even help catch the chickens that had escaped from **Backmans**.

When they walked down the streets of Waterville they could stop in the Red Top Cafe and have a Mudball, visit **Glenn's** Bake shop for a hot slice of white bread, go to **Luther's** 5 and 10 cent store where everything was 5 and 10 cents. They could take in a movie at the Gem and see *Lady and the Tramp* or, if they were more daring, they could go to a coon feed at the Corner Bar. They could buy film at **Stucky's** Pharmacy, shop for 50's groceries at **Pete's, Dusbabek's, Norman's, Comstock's** or **Dudley's**. They could have an ice cream sundae at **Courtney's** soda fountain and eat it on their white marble top tables. **Al** and **Ray's** Auto and **Greer's** Auto featured 50's autos.

Children of the parents who worked in Waterville were taught in 1950's schools. Surprisingly, they turned out as well if not better than kids taught in more progressive schools. Visitors toured the schools regularly, ate the buttered sandwiches and hamburger gravy over mashed potatoes for lunch and danced at the regular noon sock-hops in the gym.

People could step further back into history by attending The **Andrews** Opera House that was rebuilt on the north side of Lake Tetonka. The horse races and fireworks had returned. People could catch a train from downtown Waterville that would take them to the **Andrew's**. People could sit in the shade of the oaks on the bank and watch the performance on the lake. After the performance, the fireworks display would begin. The opera house was part of a historical park that featured a Waterville Historical Museum and camping area.

Many homes in the city were open to visitors to tour. People always commented about the gravel roads with pot holes and wished they had a few in their own community. Arrangements could even be made for people to live and work in the city for periods of one week to one month to really experience the 50's feeling. All citizens of Waterville were required to take courses in 50's language training.

A special attraction for visitors was the leisurely three hour ride down the Cannon River, through Lake Tetonka and Sakatah and up to Morristown. The Cannon River had been widened and dredged to allow passage of a very large and comfortable paddle boat.

Long ago in the future the skies were overcast;
but now the clouds had passed.
Long ago in the future Waterville dreamed a dream one day;
but now the dream was real.

Craig Eggers decisioned his wrestler from LeSueur 4-2. Waterville won 43-14. (1959)